SATAN'S CAULDRON

*Religious Extremism and the
Prospects for Tolerance*

Charles Goodwin

D1525673

University Press of America,® Inc.
Lanham · Boulder · New York · Toronto · Oxford

**Copyright © 2006 by
University Press of America,® Inc.**
4501 Forbes Boulevard
Suite 200
Lanham, Maryland 20706
UPA Acquisitions Department (301) 459-3366

PO Box 317
Oxford
OX2 9RU, UK

Library of Congress Control Number: 2005935693
ISBN 0-7618-3379-X (paperback : alk. ppr.)

Dedication

For Sam, who has yet to confront these questions but will have to all too soon.

There will be no peace among the nations without peace among the religions. There will be no peace among the religions without dialogue between the religious. There will be no dialogue between the religions without the investigation of the foundations of the religions.

Hans Küng

Contents

Preface

Hungarian mathematician Paul Erdös characteristically proclaimed: "My brain is open", to state that he was ready to discuss proofs. I consider these to be the most encouraging and hopeful words that can be uttered. Being open to the ideas of others and being willing to discuss them is the essence of civilization.[1]

As the world viewed from inside the industrial nations is periodically misted by uncertainty and is increasingly exposed to the lightening of unexpected evil, it will have to nurture every civilized trait. Indeed, the future of Western civilization may depend upon such nurturing, and nowhere is the call for open minds more urgent than in the realm of religious belief.

The bubble of psychological security was punctured dramatically for the United States on September 11, 2001. The ripples cascading outward from these tragedies, and the reactions to them, have altered the world's psychological and physical atmosphere. Vulnerabilities of even the most powerful have been exposed to the hate-energy of extremism, triggering white-hot chains of serial retaliation. These conditions are not new, of course. History brims with similarities that provide lessons if not comfort.

In the United States we have faced the occasional burst of militant millennialism, like the one that not so long ago was consumed in the conflagration at Waco.[2] We have experienced religious persecution of various types. We have had to contend with nations (Iran, Afghanistan) co-opted by cadres of religious extremists. But the fire and brimstone apparently summoned from a vengeful version of God on that September 11th brought home to every American the tremors possible from the force of extremist beliefs.

Apocalyptic nodes of belief can be isolated and allowed to atrophy. Ignored or encouraged, they can metastasize into the mainstream. Without transmitted knowledge these cancers can never be contained by bonds of understanding and acceptance, which permit moderation to grow. Therefore, comprehension of the emotional and intellectual phenomenon known variously as belief, faith, or religion[3] is an essential initial step toward limiting the spread of malignancy.

Throughout the centuries strains of both reasoned individualism and structured communitarianism have been filtered through religions with differing degrees of dilution. Dashes of mysticism, millennialism, or fundamentalism have been added from time to time, creating permutations and combinations of every description. Faith, either by its presence or absence, continuously impacts everyone's life. It cannot be avoided. It must be considered.

The main theme of this book is to analyze the texture of faith as it pertains to the question why for so many "conviction" about personal belief is only validated by a denial of what others believe?[4] Deeply held faith can be praiseworthy and contains obvious benefits. Unfortunately, strong belief can also be narrowly dogmatic with sinister implications. Prejudice, repression, and intolerant violence are three of them.

Aggressive assertion of conviction is not inherently bad. It can create tensions, though, particularly when invective is directed at those who adhere to other tenets. Stigmatization is invariably counterproductive, only serving the extremes and robbing the center of its voice.

Do fanaticisms and militancy loom larger for the belief systems of the future than they have for those of our immediate past? Will mitigating forces alleviate the threat of religious conflict? These and other basic questions will comprise chapter one, and set the tone for the chapters that follow.

Chapter two will explore the motivations behind several aspects of religious behavior. They will be linked to the questions posed in chapter one. The consequences of this behavior will appear in many of the chapters that follow.

Chapter three will assess the societal damage associated with intolerance. Intolerance can be both passive and aggressive. In either forum it has ramifications, which will be explored.

The interaction of absolute truth with faith will form the core of chapter four. If the vision of truth is indistinct, the quality of belief may suffer. If this vision is so vivid as to obscure alternatives, exclusion could be the result. The optimum societal balance is very delicate, and will be frequently addressed throughout this volume.

The twentieth century was an era of enormous scientific advancement. Among these accomplishments were conceptions of dimensionality that grew out of the general theory of relativity and quantum thinking. They have added new layers to the long-standing contest between science and religion. Chapter five goes into several aspects of this issue and suggests that there may be some optimistic possibilities.

Chapter six is concerned with belief systems closely linked to the world inhabited by spirits. Two examples are discussed, illustrating that these systems can be structural entities that both engender and embrace complete social orders.

There are potentials for widespread tolerance. There are also possibilities for very different environments. Chapter seven will look at some of them. They give an indication as to the direction our world is heading.

In order to access some of the more optimistic potentials, bridges will have to be built. Chapter eight will describe how they might be constructed and where they might lead.

This book is more of a personal odyssey than a theological treatise. Its purpose is to provide an analysis of how our various beliefs are likely to develop, and how the direst consequences can be avoided. I am reasonably optimistic that humanity will come to its senses and elect to follow the route towards tolerance, which leads away from lethal extremism. Although I must say some recent developments have shaken my confidence.

---

[1] For more on the life and work of Paul Erdös see: *The Man Who Loved Only Numbers*, written by Paul Hoffman and published in 1998 by Hyperion.

[2] In 1993 an offshoot of the millennial Branch Dravidians called Mount Carmel and led by David Koresh suffered many casualties in a fiery FBI attack on their fortified headquarters outside Waco, Texas.

[3] Not everyone considers these terms interchangeable. Elaine Pagels, for one, in her book *Beyond Belief*, published by Random House in 2003, expresses a view that *faith* involves a testing by experience, while *belief* has to be accepted as is. Hans Küng in his memoirs, *My Struggle for Freedom*, (William B. Eerdmans, 2002) as translated by John Bowden, had this to say on the subject: "In order to distinguish it [faith] from explicit belief in God and Christ I shall later give it the name 'faith', that is primal or fundamental trust which is by no means irrational."

[4] An outstanding example of this harsh but honestly held doctrine can be found in a document issued on August 6, 2000 and publicly released on September 5, 2000 by Cardinal Joseph Ratzinger then head of the Congregation for the Doctrine of the Faith. Headquartered in the Vatican. On April 19, 2005 Cardinal Ratzinger was elected Pope Benedict XVI. The thirty-six-page pamphlet is entitled *Dominus Iesus: On the Unicity and Salvific Universality of Jesus Christ and the Church*. It asserts as a doctrinal fact that the exclusive ecclesiastical home for the deposit of the fullness of Christian Truth lies within the Catholic Church. Certain other faiths and sects exist which are as equally doctrinally bold. As Elaine Pagels explains in her book *Beyond Belief*, this policy of exclusion to strengthen orthodoxy was taught by Irenaeus, Bishop of Lyons in the second century CE, and was subsequently promulgated by Athanasius, intermittently Bishop of Alexandria, with the support of Roman Emperor Constantine.

Acknowledgements

I want to give special thanks to Ben Eicher, Bill Babcock, Jane Lebron, and my son Charles for the time they spent reading drafts and making valuable suggestions.

Jan Rapp did her usual excellent job putting my words into comprehensible form and creating an index. Finally, those who listened patiently to my theories over the years and those who provided special inspiration deserve particular gratitude.

Introduction

One event galvanized my desire to write this book. That was the controversy surrounding the release of Mel Gibson's motion picture, "The Passion of The Christ." What people thought that this film said to them reflected their own fears and biases. The perceptions ranged over the spectrum of human emotions. Many of the reactions, both positive and negative, were profound; some encouraged tolerance, some urged the opposite.

Prior to this event, ideas, questions, data and snippets of prose rattled around in my brain and on bits of paper. Then they came together in this personal journey to find where we are and where we are going. More than anything else then, the ensuing pages constitute an individual road map designed to point the way towards peace of mind while navigating the minefields of religion.

Historically there have been cycles, or waves, of belief sweeping across the globe. Intensity, depth, and breadth have varied. Recently, after a period of relative calm, expressions of faith have burst into flame, igniting the ardor of fundamentalists in many belief systems. This development doesn't automatically signal a dearth of fresh ideas. In fact, at the most unlikely moments theological creativity seems to have bubbled. "The crisis of the later Middle Ages did not distract the intellectuals from theory and creativity. On the contrary, the gloom and doom of the times made them think all the more deeply about the nature of God, the universe, mankind, and society."[1] What applied to the European Middle Ages has also been true for other faiths in other eras.

Currently the world's religions are on the move. Almost before our eyes they are reacting to both internal and external pressures by forming new shapes. These new configurations have two consistencies: brittle and liquid.

Brittle consistencies tend to develop among members of long established faiths. For example, there are Anglicans and Lutherans. Both of those belief systems face the prospect of shattering over divisive issues such as homosexuality, abortion, or female clergy. Rival camps, sometimes categorized as liberals and conservatives, amass their forces armed with ultimatums and passages from scripture, ready to do battle, heedless of the consequences. The consequences could well include fragmentation.

Dynamically expanding belief systems (Pentecostals, and the Church of Jesus Christ of Latter Day Saints [Mormons] come to mind) can become liquid while flowing into new territory powered by their ability to coat without washing away existing underlying faith. This characteristic previously flourished, for example, during the growth of the Spanish and British colonial empires.

Within our own national existence we have witnessed the repercussions from these two consistencies. Protestantism has splintered continually since it first came to our shores in the early seventeenth century. These splits partially reflect preexisting fissures, but more frequently were freshly developed in our country. One instance was the Second Great Awakening, which began in about 1825. Evangelical Presbyterianism (itself an offshoot of Congregationalism) spread like a raging torrent through the Northeast and Mid-Atlantic in a gusher lasting for over thirty years. Led by evangelist Charles Grandison Finney it particularly appealed to the urban poor and lower middle class, who were seeking validation for their lives. This was one of the most intensely religious periods the country has ever experienced.

Sometimes new configurations lead to extremism, buttressed by strong convictions that aggressively project certainty. These convictions are often strengthened by the nationalism or frustrations of those whose worldview seems eclipsed or marginalized by the encroachment of materialism or moral laxity. The appeal of these convictions is enhanced by a clarity and simplicity of message, which can slice easily through the gentle but often fuzzy tones of moderation.

Extremism reverberates like a clap of thunder in our world. These echoes create an environment in which moderates seem to be losing their voice. Scrambling to maintain their equilibrium, they often are overmatched oratorically and doctrinally by their focused and articulate rivals. This situation has brought with it a greater proclivity for intolerance, exclusion, and violence.

Also accompanying militant extremism is stigmatization. It can cover a wide swath of territory in emotionally charged times such as we have now. Consequently it can promote misunderstanding and division where connections once prevailed. By its very nature stigmatization is the archenemy of understanding.

It is a challenge for our era to discover ways to defuse militant extremism before its concussions reverberate any further. This book will discuss the causes, the concussions, and also possible buffers. Democracy is one remedy that is touted in this country. With its emphasis upon the dialogue of exchanged views it certainly can be a valuable instrument of temperance. But democracy can only be effective if it can be molded to the conditions of each new environment. A "one size fits all" mentality, which insists upon exporting a particular variety, will not likely succeed, especially in the area of religion. The future of our world may depend upon discovery and application of the appropriate formula for offering democracy and accepting the various forms in which it emerges.

No symbol of evil, be it called Satan, or Mephistopheles, or Beelzebub[2], could conjure up a more ferocious scenario than ones involving jet planes crashing into the World Trade Center, terrorists blowing themselves up in population centers, or bombs crashing into civilian habitations. Most of these horrors can be traced to intense belief. If our civilization is to escape the heat radiating from Satan's cauldron it will have to develop understanding and build bridges. Otherwise, the forces already unleashed may become too powerful to contain. Moderation standing against extremism is not a new story. Most of the time extremism delivers fierce blows, gains some initial ground, and then is absorbed by the gradually enveloping folds of moderation. The story of this century will determine whether this pattern will hold, or how it will differ.

During the course of this effort I have come to understand that one of the reasons why I undertook this project was to discover, uncover, or reaffirm my own beliefs. In this regard the research and the required introspection invested in it have been enormously personally helpful. The results of my personal quest will be evident in the ensuing pages. It has enhanced my own knowledge and understanding. Hopefully, a bit of that will rub off on others.

---

[1] Norman F. Cantor, *The Civilization of the Middle Ages*, (New York: Harper Collins, 1993), p. 529.

[2] Satan was the traditional opponent of God or Jesus in Judeo-Christian literature. He was variously portrayed as a rebellious angel, a personal temptor of Jesus, a personification of heresy, and the ruler of Hell. As Iblis he was cast as an evil figure in Islam, as was Satan in the Judeo-Christian ethos.

Beelzebub in the Old Testament was identified as the god of the Philistine city of Ekron. In the New Testament he was called the "prince of this world," and the opposite of the true God who is the source of all good.

Mephistopheles was the devil that purchased the soul of Dr. Faustus (in Christopher Marlowe's play) or Faust (in Goethe's play).

Chapter One

Questions

The partisan, when he is engaged in a dispute, cares nothing about the rights of the question, but is anxious only to convince his bearers of his own assertions.

Socrates

In an effort to explore how we construct our belief systems this book focuses on one critical question as its central theme: Why is it that for so many the validity of their beliefs can only be sustained by denying the beliefs of others? This question gets at the essence of the prospects for religious tolerance in our world. Without a willingness to accept others' beliefs as inherently valid, tolerance will be difficult to achieve. Acceptance will only follow understanding.

This one basic question gives rise to clusters of others, which involve issues all of us have to confront on a daily basis. This chapter will discuss these clusters. However, answers, to the extent that there are any, and discussion will for the most part be reserved for the chapters that follow.

CERTAINTY

One of religion's main functions, perhaps its most basic, is to provide a foundation of certainty to which people can anchor. Most relish such a haven from the tempestuous uncertainties that batter them from so many directions. In fact, as the outside environment becomes increasingly stressful, the desire to cling to bedrock grows even more fervid, even if it should stray over the border into irrationality.

Unfortunately, the world doesn't always cooperate. Philosophical and scientific developments create a shifting ground, upsetting emotional or intellectual balance. A person failing to regain balance will reach out to grasp for presumed certainties, even if this act should lead to intolerance. Thus, the cluster of questions arising from the need for certainty is particularly poignant. The first one is whether there is such a thing as absolute truth. Most belief systems seemed to be based upon it. But does espousal of a religious belief as being an "absolute truth" have to deny that someone else's sincerely held religious belief of "absolute truth" can be valid for them? Can there be several concepts of truth bundled together or coexisting side by side? At what point does strong belief become presumed truth? Most importantly, we need to ask whether a concept of truth has to be Mithraic[1], or can it encompass gray areas?

The light and dark of Mithraic conviction arrived on these shores with the first Puritan settlers in New England and has remained an important element of our culture down to the present day. A characterization of Jefferson is as applicable some current political figures as it was to those of his generation. "Here was the classic Jeffersonian vision…it always came down to the forces of light against the forces of darkness with no room for anything in between."[2] If the tendency to grasp for certainties creates a light and dark world, how can one relate to ideas that are apparently contrary without practicing intolerance or discrimination? When transposed to social contracts and geopolitics this becomes a critical question.

How can the certainties of different faiths be compared? A glance at Hinduism's pursuit of truth reveals some similarities, and some differences, with Western belief systems.

> The infinite is down in the darkest profoundest vault of our being, in the forgotten well-house, the deep cistern. What if we could bring it to light and draw from it unceasingly? This question became India's obsession. Her people sought religious truth not simply to increase their store of general information; they sought it as a chart to guide them to higher states of being.[3]

Is this desire for truth benign enough to be accepted by other faiths, or is it enough of a threat to induce persecution, warranted or not?

Metaphysical goals, such as salvation, paradise, or nirvana, have always been lightening rods for certainty. In fact, they are often seen as unattainable without it. Since these sometimes-diaphanous concepts lie at the heart of emotional security, they can arouse a fierce defense whenever the veracity of their accepted truths is questioned. That very fierceness prompts questions about the ties between metaphysics and certainty. Can they exist? Should their nebulous intellectual state induce tolerance? Or does metaphysics promote definitional difficulty that by itself creates dangerous possessiveness?

Another certainty issue revolves around what is or is not ineffable. Many faiths have proclaimed God unknowable, and have employed conceptual intermediaries. Strains of Christianity fall into that category. But how are these groups to be regarded by those more distinct, even anthropomorphic visions of the divine? Where does reason apply and where does unquestioning belief take over? These are ancient disputes, which incorporate the philosophy of ideas as part of their weapons arsenal.[4]

Platonists (and neo-Platonists) held that ideas were reality. As we will discover when these pages unfold, "reality" is not easy to define. How does one pose questions about belief? Plato's teacher, Socrates, raised the art of questioning to an art form. Dialogue formed the basis for large blocks of the Christian foundation well into the Middle Ages. And yet, questioning can be viewed as anathema in matters of religion, to the point of being dangerous. What should the role of questions be within belief systems? What type of reaction is to be expected and is "reality" too individual a concept to be relevant?

Faiths employ different means to assist in the attainment of conviction. These can involve anthropomorphism, celibacy, mortification of the flesh, isolation, and hallucinogens. Do such encouraged, guided, or enforced means weaken in any way the results produced? If one disapproves of either the means or the ends of a quest for truth, is tolerance precluded?

A great majority of us acknowledge some fear of the cosmic unknown that surrounds death. Many of us accept that there have to be unknowables. Most of us have developed mechanisms for handling that which we cannot know or cannot understand. One of these mechanisms is religion. To some belief systems certainty is a necessity. Can these religions coexist with people for whom certainty is less essential? Whatever the answer, certainty, its challengers, and its modifiers lie at the core of any religious interaction.

MYTH [5]

We have already brushed up against the conundrum that accuracy or believability in the mind of one person might appear completely differently to another. In the area of myth this question rises to a whole new level. Belief systems often have a myth somewhere at their core. It may involve creation. It may involve an individual. Often the difference between myth and reality is indistinguishable. As such, myth can become essential to the integrity of individual or collective belief.

Then what about history? Is there a value in the careful analysis of history to separate it from myth? Does it matter whether believers revere mythological events or individuals without historical substantiation? Can whatever exists within a person's mind validly constitute individual "reality"? As academic methodology has improved, these questions have become more relevant, if not more answerable. Discovering the historical reality of Jesus, Mohammed, Buddha, or Zarathushtra has become almost as consuming to some as deciphering the meaning contained in religious texts by or about them. But the shards of history rarely match the essence of faith, causing confusion and dispute.

Throughout recorded history, religious belief systems at times have attributed divine characteristics to their revered figures. Occasionally this has led to mythic characters being worshipped as divine. Additionally, Divine Beings in some religious belief systems have been accorded mythic qualities, activities, or achievements. One result of this mixing of myth and divinity has been the production of a larger number of worshippers. Another result is that for millennia what some have perceived as myth and others as history has provided a sheltering blanket of hope against the world's insecurities. Perhaps the whole myth-history question should dissolve into acceptance.

Those seeking absolutes bridle at acceptance, their beliefs, myths or not, are not open to question. But even those most dedicated to certainties tend to find relativism in both history and myths. The belief systems of religious groups, even those containing what might be myths, are relatively sited in particular cultural contexts. Their accepted truths, even those perceived as absolute when viewed from inside, can be subjective when viewed from outside. Failure to acknowledge this situation can lead to intolerance. Intolerance can be more extreme in the area of myth; where historical proof takes a holiday.

MYSTICISM

Mysticism is defined as "a spiritual discipline aiming at direct union or communion with God." Virtually every religion has at least one mystical element. Some religions are more heavily laden than others with mystical overtones, and therefore attract controversy. For instance, one religion may advocate union with God, a feat those of other faiths deny as even being possible. By encouraging personal relationships with God mysticism can bypass established religious hierarchies, obviously challenging their power. Mystic systems are often charismatic[6], which can also be controversial.

But mysticism survives, even thrives, in difficult times because it offers hope to individuals that God cares. The intensity of this caring can be more focused than is the case in non-mystical faiths. What this says about the relationship of God to man varies. Indeed, mystic power oscillates between security and rootlessness. What should God be asked to provide? Is the mystic connection evidence of an afterlife? Can God actually be part of individual humans? Can individuals be a part of God?

The mystic world can contain visions, time travel, and dream travel, among other things. It raises questions about the nature of differences between a spiritual world and the one we appear to inhabit daily. Is the mystic world occasional or permanent? Can mysticism interact with established religion? If so what would be its role? How does a mystical approach affect the interpolation of basic texts?

Mysticism can span the emotional spectrum. Iran, for example, has a history where different types of mysticism have been evident. Two examples are illustrative. Jalaluddin Rumi lived from 1207-1273 CE, in present day Iran, Afghanistan, and Turkey. He was a Sufi[7] who wrote some of the most beautiful poetry the world has ever seen. The majority of it expressed a mystical, intensely romantic involvement with God. The mystic Ayatollah Ruhollah Khomeni founded the Islamic Republic of Iran in 1979, instituting a strict, puritanical, often militant regime. He fostered a society that has been both admired and feared, but its influence has radiated. Both of these men were well known mystics confronting established political and religious entities. They illustrate how mysticism can emerge in different forms, and can lead in a multiplicity of directions, even defying or becoming government.

History has demonstrated that as events grow grimmer, the world is likely to become mystical. Mysticism can be deeply embedded. How can government, institutions, and individuals deal with it? How can it be acknowledged and accepted? Mysticism is often influential without being overwhelming. How is it to be regarded? These are complexities presented by the mystic world, but there is little evidence that the mystic world itself considers these complexities as relevant. If mysticism continues to spread, all of us will have to come to terms with it, in one way or another.

ALTERNATIVES

Religious, or quasi-religious, belief systems can assume many shapes and can involve a wide variety of practices. Sometimes these forms are difficult for others to understand or accept.

Intellectual circles seem wary of the New Age, and academic studies of alternative spirituality, especially ones based on first-hand experience, are surprisingly scarce. One academic found her colleagues less than supportive.

> After hearing about my research, for example, a psychologist remarked, 'I don't know how you can spend time with these sickening New Age types. They're just rich people with too much time on their hands.' Her opinion was only slightly more caustic than offered by other university colleagues. None would think of making such disparaging comments about the religious beliefs of the Yoruba, the Hopi, or the Australian aborigines.[8]

Many belief systems, or sects, begin as alternatives to what is considered orthodoxy. It is often the case, and understandably so, that they are regarded most suspiciously within the confines of the systems with which they have the greatest degree of similarity. Unfortunately suspicion sometimes begets persecution when difference is perceived as threat.

As a religion develops, often so do her prodigal children, who leave home for other explorations. Then, as one branch establishes itself as orthodoxy, repression is all too often employed to repel challenges to this new position. It has been an age-old question for believers confronting alternatives to determine how they will react to different faiths, different interpretations, or even to different religious ideas. Should they be welcomed, tolerated, ignored, or feared? Ironically, it may be easier to have a benign reaction if one doesn't take the other faith too seriously. Certainly, it is easier to be tolerant if one doesn't feel one's own spiritual equilibrium to be threatened.

The present day seems to be generating an unusual degree of motion within and among belief systems. Some of this movement creates layering upon orthodox bases. Offshoots are sprouting with regularity. New concepts are being floated. Reactionism abounds. As a result, it is becoming harder for people to locate reliable religious landmarks, which makes them question all the more, sometimes harshly.

The issues of landmarks and reactions vary from faith to faith. Within Christianity, for example, philosophers have tended to be the bastions of orthodoxy, whereas changes, alternatives, and heterodoxies have largely come from clerics. Within Islam the situation has been reversed, as philosophers have inspired evolutions or revolutions.[9] Where these developments come from in each belief system can determine the direction and the nature of the reaction.

Fundamentalists are usually perceived as the least forgiving towards alternatives, especially within their own belief systems. Proselytizers by definition are dedicated to changing the beliefs of others. Atheists are the opponents of belief itself. Even where these stereotypes prevail they all must tread a fine line in their attitudes towards alternatives. If questions become, or are taken to be, threats, they can easily provoke intolerance.

Crosscurrents from politics or secular policy can roil previously calm waters. As the surface turns to waves, or static crackles in the air, questions from or about alternatives can turn hostile. Seeking a tranquil atmosphere for dialogues can be the most important quest. Questions can so easily turn into challenges. Alternatives can be perceived as threats. Tolerance requires effort. Understanding takes willpower. Ecumenism may require emotional security, but at the very least it requires restraint.

TIMING

Time, even metaphysical time, plays an important role in religion. Rebirth, a return to earthly existence for a divine figure, or salvation coming in different forms at different points are all features of some religious belief systems. What can happen, and when it can happen, varies from system to system, but nonetheless each variation contains a degree of significance for members. This significance has a relationship with some facet of time.

Many belief systems have grown up around the provision of rewards during life. Some venerate material achievement. Others focus upon abstractions, both earthly and ethereal. *When* one is "saved" can command a degree of importance rivaling *how* or *where*. Of course, grasping at temporal solace can be put down to expediency. But questions about timing can be critical for internal security.

Greek philosophers raised a related series of questions. Was immortality individual (Plato), or communal (Aristotle)? Their answers influenced the qualities of where and when. They also began to consider infinity (Archimedes) and eternity (Plato), both affecting the timing of belief. In a slight variation on the old adage, "timing is everything", these philosophers began a journey towards human belief, which has continued to grapple with timing issues right down to the present day.

The book of *Revelation* has been enormously influential within Christianity. Its visions of the Apocalypse have inspired a multitude of sects and systems. In many respects the questions it raises are more significant than the contents of any answers.

At the same time, most Christians have made God a partner in their daily lives, developing various mechanisms of access. These mechanisms are closely allied to various attributes of timing. They address timing. They punctuate timing. In some instances they are the timing. Questions about timing are an important part of the delicate process that shapes belief systems and their application to individuals.

DIMENSIONALITY

Questions raised by the many ramifications of dimensionality can affect they way we believe. In the early part of the twentieth century Albert Einstein published his ideas about a fourth dimension, which he called spacetime. Many others have built upon this concept. One of these constructs has led to the string and superstring theories of existence, which employ the technique of multidimensionality.

Multidimensionality could be in conflict with ideas about absolute truth, although its antecedent spacetime was itself conceived as an absolute. It is hard enough to understand the world from the perspective of three dimensions. Additional dimensionality is an intellectual and perceptual complication. The mere fact that these dimensions could exist may assist the cause of tolerance, just by raising questions. Conversely, they could make it harder, merely by sowing the seeds of confusion which in turn encourages rigidity.

The biggest question of all, as well as the biggest answer, because it is the most solid bridge between science and faith, may be the uncertainty principle. Developed in 1927 by physicist Nils Bohr's protégé Werner Heisenberg, the uncertainty principle formed a cornerstone of quantum theory, which was just then beginning to emerge[10]. Essentially it held that one could only be certain about any factor or reaction when it was actually under observation. The rest of the time it was unknown. Regarded from the viewpoint of religion this principle indicates that science, no matter how sophisticated, can never have all the answers. There will always be unknowns, hence leaving room for God in even the most rigorous scientific discipline. One cannot escape questions, but interestingly enough the ones left in place by the uncertainty principle may point the way toward tolerance.

FORMATIONS

Religion, as always, is experiencing transition and reconfiguration. Presently, both of these processes may be in a dramatic phase. Existing faiths are taking on new shapes, or layers. New faiths, hybrids and originals, are emerging. Individual congregations are dividing and reforming. Conjecture about a belief system map for this century thus opens the door to many questions, and these questions are dealing with moving targets.

How many of these faiths will be fundamentalist, or millennialist? Will the tides of mysticism roll in once more? How will these emerging systems compare to those of the last century? Will belief and government be more or less connected that they are today? These questions, and more, throb ever more loudly.

Are the conditions are right for a new Axial Age to form? Running roughly from 800 to 200 BCE the original was a period of dynamic change. As tribal networks with their animistic beliefs coalesced into more complex societies, religion kept pace. In fact, many faiths (for example: Buddhism, Taoism, Confucianism, Judaism, Hinduism and Zoroastrianism) came together and spread during this period. The Axial Age was, even more that the Renaissance, a period of turmoil and creativity.

Although there were numerous stretches of civil strife, there was also a remarkable degree of religious tolerance as polities were formed. Is such a period, a new Axial Age, underway right now? What will be forming and what will be changing? Are major new belief systems gestating?

How things turn out may depend upon the ability to question what is established. Faiths can arise from a blizzard of questions. As a faith matures, and its dogma is solidified, questioning what has been established can be seen as an explicit threat. Once questions are repressed other forms of intolerance become more likely. Measuring the fluidity of belief and the ability to question will become an important gauge of the prospects for tolerance.

---

[1] Mithraism originated in the Vedic culture of Central and South Asia. It became a belief system in the first or second century Roman Empire probably in the area that is present day Iran. Mithraism followed the Zoroastrian practice of dividing the universe into light (good) and dark (evil). Mithra was a sun god, and the epitome of good. It continued a long tradition existing in philosophy and belief, which attempted to divide essential forces into two competing entities.

[2] Joseph J. Ellis, *Founding Brothers: The Revolutionary Generation* (New York, Alfred A. Knopf, 2001), p. 231.

[3] Houston Smith, *The World's Religions* (Harper Collins, New York, 1991), p. 26.

[4] For some recent explorations of the reason and faith issue see:

   Richard Dawkins, *A Devil's Chaplain* (Houghton Mifflin)
   Robert Fogelin, *Walking the Tightrope of Reason* (Oxford University Press)
   Charles Freeman, *The Closing of the Western Mind* (Alfred A. Knopf)
   Jennifer Michael Hecht, *Doubt: A History* (Harper Collins)
   Alan Wolfe, *The Transformation of American Religion* (Free Press)

[5] After completing a draft of this section, I was urged to read Otto Rank's, *The Myth and Birth of the Hero*, which could provide greater depth of understanding. It was well worth reading, and the section has been reworked.

[6] Charisma can denote a magnetic personality, frequently a trait of mystic leaders. It can also describe emotional spontaneity in outlook and practice, another mystic trait.

[7] Sufis, the name is derived from the Arabic definition for "wool wearer", are Islamic mystics both ascetic and gnostic. Their rituals are cloaked in secrecy and dependent upon the particulars of each sect. Each sect in turn is influenced by the teachings of its founder.

Over the years Sufis have been persecuted by orthodox Islam, which often perceives Sufis to be a threat.

[8] Michael F. Brown, *The Channeling Zone: American Spirituality in an Anxious Age* (Cambridge: Harvard University Press, 1997) p. 9-10.

[9] A valuable explanation of this condition can be found in *History of Islamic Philosophy*, edited by Seyyed Hossein Nasr and Oliver Leaman, and published in 1996 by Routledge in London.

[10] A good readable summary of these ideas can be found in Brian Greene's book, *The Elegant Universe* (New York: Alfred A. Knopf, 2004). On page 79 of that book Greene sums up the quantum situation with its inherent uncertainty principle. "Quantum mechanics breaks with this tradition. We *can't* ever know the exact location and exact velocity of even a single particle. We *can't* predict with total certainty the outcome of even the simplest of experiments, let alone the evolution of the entire cosmos. Quantum mechanics shows that the best we can ever do is predict the *probability* that an experiment will turn out this way or that."

Chapter Two

Motivations

He [Harrison] does not indicate what he means by the word 'scandal' [in 'scandal of death'], but I would guess following his train of thought, it is the opposite of an acceptance of death as a part of the natural order, and instead is the sense of death as an insult, an outrage, shocking both individual sensual life and the continuity of social and moral community.

W. S. Merusin, in a review of Robert Pogue Harrison's, *The Dominion of the Dead*, in *The New York Review of Books* April 8, 2004

The motivations for belief are an important factor in determining the prospects for tolerance. There are motivations for the existence of religion. There are motivations for each shade of every faith. Within the envelope of belief there are pressures and insecurities that create attitudes. Often the line separating some version of tolerance and the onset of discrimination is extremely fine. Sometimes it is hard to discern precisely why some believers feel that only by disparaging the convictions of others can their own convictions be validated. However, a close inspection of motivations may yield some clues.

This chapter is built around a study of three basic motivations, along with several sub-categories. Unsurprisingly, these motivations reveal that belief arises from our most basic instincts. These instincts are not always benign. That fact is not shocking. But what can be shocking at times are the uses to which some of these instincts are occasionally dedicated. It is not pre-ordained that human beings have to be malicious towards one another. Most faiths specifically counsel against such behavior. Nonetheless, all too often people drift into patterns of intolerance, even active discrimination against one another.

FEAR

Fear manifests itself in various guises within the human psyche. Consequently it produces a variety of reactions. In this section we will address six distinct but frequently related manifestations. Each of them can drive our behavior. In combinations they can turn malignant.

Fear of Death

Fear of death is perhaps the primal human emotion, lodged deep within the only species that knows it will eventually die.[1] Stephan Alter describes the faith-inducing fear that gripped him while ensconced in a tent during a Himalayan storm.

> Fear is often the raw material of faith and it takes different forms, from momentary panic to prolonged anxiety. Many times I have felt afraid for no reason at all, an irrational nervousness that makes me keep glancing over my shoulder as I walk through a forest. But that night at Panwali (in the Himalayas) there was nothing ambiguous about the fear I experienced. Each bolt of lightening sent a current of terror through my body and as I lay there in the tent I felt the immediate possibility of death. At the same time there was an excitement to the storm, so powerful it was oppressive and almost erotic, my mind filled with horrifying visions of electricity surging through my body. Worst of all were those moments of anticipation between each thunderclap, waiting for the next flash of light to fuse earth and sky. My nerves were like copper wires threaded throughout my bones, a circuitry of fear. They ran from the base of my skull between each vertebra in my back and into my joints, through the hollow crater of each socket and down to my toes and fingers. Every time the lightening struck the tension increased, as if my nerves were twisting inside bones. Lying there on my back with my eyes closed I could understand the terror the gujjar girl (Muslim buffalo herder) had felt the night before, a paralyzing sense of hysteria brought on by the volatility of nature. Even when the storm eventually subsided, more than an hour later, I could not escape the residual fears that kept me awake for most of the night. In the silence that followed the storm I experienced an uneasy reverence for the ferocity of wind and weather.[2]

The great Swedish warrior King Gustavus Adolphus put it tersely: "the fear of death, which is the greatest fear of all".[3] He was well aware of it, having faced death dozens of times. He finally received a mortal wound at the age of 38 on the battlefield of Lutzen while in command of the Protestant armies who, in 1632, achieved their greatest victory of the Thirty Years' War against the Catholic forces.

Fear of death accompanied by a certain excitement, or by the encompassing dread of unknown emptiness, or by the long awaited ecstasy of reunion with the divine, can circulate within us at the moment when death seems imminent.

> For all peoples death is the first teacher, the first pain, the edge beyond which life as we know it ends and wonder begins Death's essence is the severance from the mortal body of some elusive life-giving principle, and how a culture comes to understand or at least tolerate this inexorable separation to a great extent defines its mystical worldview.[4]

For millennia cultures have struggled to construct belief systems that would permit acceptance, even the welcoming, of death. This effort has been a driving, metaphysical force. In some cases faiths have risen or fallen based upon their successes in this area.

It can be argued that fear of death is the basis for every other emotion, dwarfing them all. It can be further contended that this single fear is the basis for most, if not all, human action. So comprehensive is it that virtually all belief systems are organized around one or more methods for dealing with the looming inevitability of death.

As one scans an encyclopedia of faiths, explanations vary for the fact of death and for the several attempts to neutralize it. Afterlives proliferate, with kaleidoscopes of attendant features. A cycle of rebirths with the potential for ultimate release is a common scenario. Unification of past and future lives via rituals, dreams, stimulants, or some combination thereof, is a frequent palliative. Use of hallucinogens, fasting or meditation can create an apparently seamless connection among present, past, future and infinity that can in effect transcend death. Belief in the eternity of the soul can temper fear. Anticipation of a welcome into divine presence can remove death's sting. The common thread is transformation of death from terrible finality to something benign, or even exalted. If we are honest with ourselves, we have to admit that we dearly desire to believe that death if not understood, at least should not be feared.

How far are we willing to go in order to obtain this release? That is a crucial question, the answer to which reveals much about any society or any civilization. Orlando Figes in his book *Natasha's Dance* addresses the preoccupation with death gripping the great Russian writers Tolstoy, Chekhov, and Dostoevsky who wrote about it to each other as well as in their work. "Tolstoy's...personal root of his religion was a fear of death, which became more intense with every passing year. Death was an obsession throughout his life and art." So catastrophic is the perceived alternative that we are prepared (as were the ancient Greeks among others) to commit all of our material and emotional resources in order to restrain the infinite waves of uncertainty swept in by the inexorable tide of our forthcoming death.[5]

Sometimes this attempt can have very unfortunate results, as history all too graphically points out. However, in certain circumstances we can condition ourselves to accept, ignore, or even court, death. Martyrdom can be one such circumstance. War, as Stephen Ambrose describes, can be another.

When men are in combat, the inevitability of it takes over. They are there; there is nothing they can do to change that, so they accept it. They immediately become callused to the smell of death, the bodies, the destruction, the killing, and the danger. Enemy bodies and wounded don't affect them. Their own wounded and the bodies of their dead friends make only a brief impression, and in that impression is a fleeting feeling of triumph or accomplishment that it was not them. There is still work to be done, a war to be won, and they think about that. Once out of the line, back in a rest camp, they remember how their friends were wounded or killed. They remember times when they were inches or seconds from their own death. Far from combat, death and destruction are no longer inevitable – the war might end, the missions might be cancelled. With these thoughts men become nervous about going back in. As soon as they are back in, however, those doubts and nervousness are gone, the callousness, the cold bloodedness, the calmness return.[6]

Martyrs and soldiers are examples of those who can occasionally inoculate themselves against a fear of death. But these examples are rare. Dread over the unknown inevitability of death is difficult to contain. But it can be modified through a structure of religious belief. Such modification is a major motivation for worship.

Allied to this constant battle against the unknown void is the ageless effort of humans to derive some significance from their lives. At the margin just staying alive is a daily contest and a source of significance in and of itself. At progressively higher levels of existence significance begins to equate with some attempt to capture eternity. The final curtain can be kept from closing by a promise of eternal light presented in one guise or another.[7]

A very basic way of avoiding the clutches of extinction is through perpetuation; have a large family with a substantial number of sons. Paintings, monuments, or eponymous corporations are additional means for perpetuating existence. Searching for some method to snatch immortality from oblivion, or ingraining belief systems that perform a similar task, can provide an alternative to, or a mitigation of, the numbing finality of death. Leon Kass categorized the growing fear of death in the modern industrial world as endemic. This fear is a fundamental emotion.

> True, many causes of death have been vanquished, but the fear of death has not abated, and many, indeed, have gotten worse. For as we have saved ourselves from the rapidly fatal illnesses, we now die slowly, painfully and in degradation – with cancer, AIDS, or Alzheimer's disease. In our effort to control and rationalize death and dying we have medicalized and institutionalized so much of the end of life as to produce what amounts to living death for thousands of people.[8]

Attempts to escape fear of death by replacing it with a paradise of heaven have sometimes induced believers to wander down unfortunate byways. Crusades, jihads and the like promise forgiveness for sins and immediate salvation to anyone perishing while physically combating individuals of differing faiths, or heterodox members of ones own. In this mindset the Almighty presumably sanctions slaughter and torture so that a particular belief system "the 'right' system" can prevail for both the perpetrator and the recipient.. If death can be construed as martyrdom it can be transformed thereby into a blessed event to be welcomed, not feared. The end result, overcoming fear, is thus achieved, using the bodies and souls of others under the banner of purifying the faith.

At the base of this militantly purifying role for belief is insecurity. "What if my faith is not enough and death really is to be feared?" "What if the other person's faith can somehow subvert mine and make me lose my protection from that awful finality?" So often intolerance in its most brutal manifestations is born out of a hunger for insulation from the fear of death rooted in insecurity.

It doesn't make any difference what medical miracles we employ or how long we actually live – the inescapable fact is that we are eventually going to die. Carlos Casteñeda expanded on this theme. "We are indeed beings that are going to die. Therefore, the real struggle of man is not the strife with his fellow men, but with *infinity*, and this is not even a struggle; it is, in essence, an acquiescence. We must voluntarily acquiesce to *infinity*."[9] We are all dying from the moment we are born. The only differences between individuals are the rate and the required adjustment. Keith Ward sums it up. "What has led many Christians to the harsh doctrine that one must belong to a particular church to be saved is their fear that the point of belonging to the church may be obscured, if one can be saved without belonging to it at all."[10] This statement can be applied to many belief systems. They have permitted their fundamental principles to be subverted into intolerance, even aggressive intolerance. This subversion can be traced to fear, most basically of death. Pierre Teilhard de Chardin characterized it graphically, "The paralyzing poison of death eats irresistibly into everything that we make – and everything that we do. Stop for a moment and inspect everything we believe, every action we take." How much of it is ultimately tied to a fear of death."[11] Isn't religion an attempt to deal with death? Best of all, of course, religion solves the problem of death, which no living individuals can solve, no matter how they would support us. Finally, religion alone gives hope, because it holds open the dimension of the unknown and unknowable."[12]

It is a primal fear that has prompted us to believe, and to cling fiercely to any cluster of tenets that promise removal of the coldness that surrounds our hearts whenever we contemplate the void that death can summon. Death is not the only fear motivating the texture of beliefs. There are others, and we will look at some of them.

Fear of Rootlessness

Most of us want to feel rooted in some way. Whether it is through family, community, faith, ethnicity, or another attachment, we crave a sense of belonging. Belonging carries with it an aura of security that not only insulates us here on earth, but also can translate into a certain kind of immortality through some version of continuity. The opposite feeling – rootlessness – is viewed with dread. When applied to the area of belief, dread can be magnified. Drifting unmoored upon a sea of doubt is a nightmare, destabilizing lives, igniting other fears, removing basic elements of humanity. The *Bible* issued a plaint that resonates throughout most belief systems: "Woe is me for I am lost."[13]

Rootlessness and the resultant insecurity are the archenemies of inner peace. Insecurities are often fought by employing structural belief systems. Václav Havel describes the function and appeal of the communist systems that descended upon Eastern Europe after World War II. Even though theoretically godless, they bore similarities with the function and appeal of many orthodox or fundamentalist belief systems.

> It commands an incomparably more precise, logically structured, generally comprehensible and, in essence, extremely flexible ideology that, in its elaborateness and completeness, is almost a secularized religion. It offers a ready answer to any questions whatsoever; it can scarcely be accepted only in part, and accepting it has profound implications for human life. In an era when metaphysical and existential certainties are in a state of crisis, when people are being uprooted and alienated and are losing their sense of what this world means, this ideology inevitably has a certain hypnotic charm. To wandering humankind it offers an immediately available home: all one has to do is accept it, and suddenly everything becomes clear once more, life takes on new meaning and all mysteries, unanswered questions, anxiety and loneliness vanish. Of course, one pays dearly for this low-rent home: the price is abdication of one's own reason, conscience, and responsibility, for an essential aspect of this ideology is the consignment of reason and conscience to a higher authority. The principle involved is that the center of power is identical with the center of truth.[14]

Even creative, freethinking people will accept an apparently restrictive structure in order to provide roots for their lives. In the search for foundation, people may seek a comprehensive system tightly bound to faith. As we will learn presently, scientists will frequently look for links between their work and faith so that they can provide philosophical or psychological answers more inwardly satisfying than those offered by science alone. There is nothing wrong with any of these actions. They are human nature. Adversities only arrive when the frenetic search for roots creates a climate for intolerance that prompts physical or psychological attacks upon others beliefs.

As people gravitate to belief systems that alleviate their sense of rootlessness, they naturally react against any action or lure that might return them to such a state. This reaction can take the form of aggressive suppression or denial of any alternative. It is not surprising that individuals or groups would cling fiercely to a set of beliefs that provides them solace. It becomes unfortunate if this grasp tightens into a fist of prejudice and repression. Belief is such an emotional expression, and it is so central to personal or collective balance, that it can lead to aggressive defense. Sometimes this can be regrettable, but it is when the emotions are channeled into offensive action that problems can escalate.

Philosopher Pierre Teilhard de Chardin calls this fear "existential fear."[15] Simply stated his antidote is a gradual unification of humankind as it evolves into more complex forms. However, this unification cannot take place unless concentration on individuality is transcended and technological limits are recognized, so that the spiritual and psychic bonds bringing humans together can strengthen. Existential fear, fear of rootlessness, can become dangerous unless the community providing security is broad enough to preclude offensively aggressive intolerance.

Our challenge both as human beings and as a civilization, is to moderate this offensive action. We are entitled, even encouraged, to seek solace from isolation in faith. We should be able to follow, hold, and defend our beliefs with conviction. We may need to enunciate and promulgate them with energy. If we denounce and punish, thus falling into the insidious grip of intolerance, we have demeaned ourselves, and the concepts we hold dear as well. But if we can recognize and accept universal connections, we have a chance to develop in relative harmony, which in the end is the strongest and most durable way to put down roots.

Fear of Belief

There is a legitimate fear of belief. However, atheists and some agnostics, often bolstered by scientific discoveries, can vehemently attack believers with invective. Because of their intensity, these battles often spill over from the realm of academia into the political sphere. As they overflow, these conflicts can affect wide swaths of any society. To say the least, they fail to qualify as legitimate expressions of non-belief and are socially counterproductive.

Atheism is a valid pursuit. But like its obverse it can be clouded by fear and hate. Some of the most fervently held tenets of belief systems seem to directly contradict the findings of science, and at the same time may challenge many building blocks of atheism.[16] Political atheism, as practiced in some forms of communism, can clash with beliefs and have socio-economic overtones. In the last half of the twentieth century the Judeo-Christian underpinnings of capitalistic Western civilization often found itself ranged against competing communistic societies which, in defiance of its almost religious ideology (noted above by Havel), trumpeted their atheism.

Belief can be perceived as a direct threat to, and thus feared by, non-belief.[17] Just as members of belief systems can fear, and strike out at, other believers who are perceived to be perniciously antithetical to their cherished principles, non-believers can feel the same pressures. They have created a worldview, or a universal view, that satisfies them. It depends upon critical premises, as does belief. But belief, which challenges the logic of these premises, can seem hostile. Conceptual hostility can readily turn to intolerance, and non-belief is not exempt from this fear-inspired disease. A reaction to this disease can be to deepen the desire to seek out the presumed comfort of certainties. This form of fear is subject to the problems certainty can create when it is not tempered by tolerance.

Fear of Divine Retribution

God is not always presented as benevolent. In Hinduism, Judaism, and Christianity, for example, the Almighty can at times be fierce and punishing. Joshua, for one, cries out: "Now, therefore fear the Lord."[18] The vengeful side of the Vedic god Shiva, and of his wife Durga, had believers trembling in fear of destruction.[19] Early Biblical writing is full of humans trembling in fear because to see God, or even personally experience God (except within the temple) was thought to mean instant death.[20] Elements of divine retribution reverberate through many belief systems. Consignment to hell, physical destruction, rebirth as a lower life form, and other punishments awaited those who offended a vengeful divine.

In the Biblical story of Moses various plagues descended upon the Egyptians who had displeased God. Another form of retribution hung over the heads of Christians in the Middle Ages:

> The classic theory was expressed by Anselm, Bishop of Canterbury (1033-1109), in his treatise *Why God Became Man*. Sin, he argues, had been an affront of such magnitude that atonement was essential if God's plans for the human race were not to be completely thwarted. The Word had been made flesh to make reparation on our behalf. God's justice demanded that he be repaid by one who was both God and man: the magnitude of the offense meant that only the Son of God could effect a salvation, but, as a man had been responsible, the redeemer also had to be a member of the human race. It was a tidy, legalistic scheme that depicted God thinking, judging weighing things up as though he were a human being. It also reinforced the Western image of a harsh God who could only be satisfied by the hideous death of his own son, who had been offered up as a kind of human sacrifice.[21]

It is all there: original sin, guilt, atonement, and the hint of retribution. The Middle Ages was also a time when disasters were attributed to a displeased God. It was not unusual during this period of time for dissenters and non-believers to face harsh persecution – even to the point of death, with their torments depicted as a rightful exercise of a temporal form of divine punishment.

What would believers do to avoid sanction, destruction, or eternal damnation? The answer was, and is, almost anything. It is not surprising, then, for us to see those who fear divine retribution reacting harshly against faiths that appear to threaten their system of beliefs or their God.

Millennialists can provide an extreme example of this characteristic. Many of them believe that they have been chosen by God to survive the apocalypse. They feel that by exercising certain elements of belief they will emerge unscathed while unbelievers are consumed. In the case of the Mandaean Gnostics the divine punishment is a world of joyless darkness for sinners and followers of other religions.[22] These punishment centers for non-believers in every level of heaven – punishment through suffering for impurity or sin.[23] Members of this faith believe that the world will be a better place when purified and inhabited by the chosen, acting with God's blessing. Other millennialists have differing tableaux, but a similar end. The world will be purified of sinful believers, and the chosen will survive alongside God.

Even when such feelings are not outwardly hostile they highlight a fragile condition. Within most people there is a churning storm of belief. Feelings of fear and compassion are waging a battle for space inside the innermost recesses of us all. How this struggle is settled, how fear of divine retribution is handled, can determine the likelihood of tolerance.

One factor previously alluded to, is perception of God. Compassionate, stern, living, vengeful, forgiving, angry; all these, and more, are divine characteristics emerging from the spectrum of faiths, or even existing within single belief systems. The traits that predominate determine reactions of believers. Blends of fear and love are common, whether religions are polytheistic or have a multifaceted and moody deity. Not all conceptions of the divine are full of compassion and love.[24] A stern, vengeful God can start adherents quaking.

Many belief systems need the presence of a figure like Satan, or a simultaneous avowal of both heaven and hell to clarify a system of punishments and rewards. The prince of the netherworld is often held over sinners as an instrument of retribution. But the presence of evil can serve as instructive fear if it is accompanied by a willingness to understand and to tolerate. When views of different faiths degenerate into fear of eternal damnation that leads to hatred of others, obviously this imagery is destructive.

Benedict of Nursia composed the Benedictine Rules around 510 CE[25] In this initial outline of monastic life he advocated an ambiance of remarkable tolerance. Had his rules been heeded and broadly observed, the development of Christianity in the Middle Ages might have been different. There might have been more compassion. Fear of divine retribution might have been less inherent in the Judeo-Christian tradition. Generations following this tradition might have regarded their fellow human beings more kindly.

Fear Of and From Persecution

Ever since the beginning of recorded history, and undoubtedly before, the tragedy of people being persecuted for their religious beliefs has recurred persistently. No belief system is exempt. Persecution itself originates from insecurity. That insecurity can result from envy of people who are more economically successful. It can stem from threatened rise of those who occupy a socio-economic basement. It can stigmatize persons who are different in appearance or dress, and that difference itself is perceived as some sort of threat. It can endow all members of a particular belief category with the characteristics of its most extreme elements. This attitude can carry over into apprehension about rituals and practices, which are unfamiliar, and therefore threatening. Persecution of others can follow repudiations of a given belief system. There are many reasons for persecution. But they all stem from fear. In turn they transmit fear. The desired result of conformity often turns to defiance, which can end tragically.

Whatever the reason, the prospect of persecution strikes fear. That fear can spur pre-emptive actions or persecution. Basically, god(s) have to succeed to survive. Rain dances have to produce rain often enough to warrant being repeated. Prayers have to be answered, some of the time, in some form, for the god(s) to whom the prayers were addressed, not to be discarded for others.[26]

The divinity figure being worshipped in a belief system can ill afford to face the possibility that it might prove incapable or woefully ineffective. Even worse, a competing system might be lurking nearby waiting to move in and overwhelm with logic, or charisma, or brute force. Those insecurities can lead to intolerance, and to violence.[27]

The more severe the divine punishment inherent in any given religion the more it may have a tendency toward violent persecution. Hundreds of millions have been slaughtered throughout the ages because others disagreed with or feared their beliefs. Hundreds of million more were actively persecuted. These actions resulted from, and resulted in, fear, based upon insecurity over salvation. On the other hand, there have been moments in history when remarkable tolerance prevailed. Maria Rosa Menocal describes one such moment.

> This [eighth to tenth century Spain] was the chapter of Europe's culture when Jews, Christians, and Muslims lived side-by-side and, despite their intractable differences and enduring hostilities, nourished a complex culture of tolerance, and it is this difficult concept that my subtitle aims to convey. This only sometimes included guarantees of religious freedoms comparable to those we would expect in a modern, 'tolerant' state; rather, it found expression in the often unconscious acceptance that contradictions – within oneself, as well a within one's culture – could be positive and productive.[28]

Ironically, this period of tolerance was immediately followed by two fundamentalist, intolerant Muslim dynasties, the Almoravids (1085-1170) and the Almohads (1171-1350). These dynasties were succeeded (in 1492) by the relatively repressive Christian kingdom of Ferdinand and Isabella. All three of the ruling cadres who succeeded the Iberian ornament engaged in widespread persecution that forced expulsions and conversions, as well as deaths. They felt the power of their faiths threatened by the presence of alternate belief systems. Iberia never again attained the level of cultural and intellectual prominence that it achieved in the eighth through tenth centuries.

Fear of Materialism

Another fear that has both created and prompted intolerance is the fear of what I call human materialism.[29] A great many faiths have eschewed the material accumulations and embraced relative if not abject poverty. Others have gone even further deciding to renounce the human corpus entirely in an attempt to be embraced by their spiritual essence and become one with it.

Monks and holy men for millennia have abandoned all possessions and wandered dependently poor among the populace. Frequently they alarm establishment hierarchies whose authority is based upon the materialism they deplore. These hierarchies often persecute or defame mendicants of their own or other faiths that, while upholding fundamental principal, present an all too visible alternative. Spiritual Franciscans are only one of thousands of groups to suffer this fate for their perceived threat. Even during the lifetime of Saint Francis of Assisi (1181-1226), but especially after it, those friars attempting to follow his example by renouncing their possessions drew down upon themselves the wrath of members of their own and other orders. No matter how pure their designs, monks who embrace poverty shake the pillars of establishment causing waves of trepidation.

Dressed in rags and holding begging bowls, permanently inhabiting pillars (sometimes turning so as always to face the sun), enduring self-exile in caves, or following a number of other rigors, those proclaiming disdain for material values, even for existence itself, can at once be sources of both adoration and scorn. Followers adore while established leaders scorn.

Many Ethiopian Copts of today, for example, believe that the weaker the body the stronger the spirit. Some of their monks deliberately reduce the human body by rigorous fasting. They regularly stand in prayer for days at a time, leaning on T-shaped staffs. These vigils are designed to induce visions that create direct communication with God. These monks are venerated as holy and wise, but simultaneously are actively persecuted as destabilizers of the Coptic status quo. As with Saint Francis, tenets once honored as spiritually admirable later can be vilified as dangerously heterodox. Even Buddhists belonging to one of the few remaining faiths to cherish poverty have experienced changes. Although many of the devout still spend brief periods of their lives as monks, the fear of materialism is waning. A desire to accumulate is on the rise.

Whenever a particular article or system of belief generates insecurity in others (especially if these others are part of an establishment cadre) the reaction can be visceral, even vicious. With both sides claiming to represent the true spirit of God and epithetical cries of heresy flying to and fro, intolerance is likely to follow.[30] In every era, in every religion, the holiness of poverty and mortification has occasionally engendered envious fear in those who hold power. Even Ghandi was not exempt. But in the age of capitalism anti-materialism can be a particular heinous offense, especially as many faiths are actively encouraging materialism.

New born again Christian churches that venerate wealth are springing up all over the United States. They have banished the fear of materialism, substituting other fears which maybe equally pernicious. Tragedy is created by fear. It can concentrate insecurity, annealing a razor sharp blade poised for plunging into the breast of any opponent. The greater the challenge to any system of beliefs, the more virulently intolerant the response can be. Rationality is exorcised by faith, frequently for good, sadly sometimes for ill. That is the intolerant legacy of fear.

POWER

The tentacles and temptations of power can wrap themselves around the corpus of any faith and directly induce expressions of intolerance. There are many tentacles with adverse characteristics. We will discuss three general areas.

But in all of them the perceived need for some type of power impels people to deny the beliefs of others, often with distressing consequences.

Emotional Power

What exactly is emotional power? It sounds a bit like love. It also resembles a type of psychological dominance. Both are somewhat accurate in describing how the concept is employed here.

If the divine bestows favor upon, or is perceived to exist within certain individuals or groups, that condition conveys emotional power. This person, or these persons, be they clergy or philosophers, in some way seek to represent the divinity. Any reception of divine recognition, or incarnation of divinity within, demonstrates a power not available to others.

These chosen or manifest leaders possess emotional power that uplifts them while creating a hold over those not similarly blessed or conferred. Emotional power *per se* may not be harmful. How it is recognized and used will determine its impact. The effort to retain and to preserve the special honor often results in active intolerance. If, for example, it is believed that not just honor but salvation is at stake, some would go to great lengths to keep divine favor from being subverted by supposed believers, even to the point of resorting to violence. This is the emotional power conferred by divinity. It can turn lethal on occasions when some feel that their own eternal existence is threatened by those who believe differently.

Emotional power, or the quest for it, can erupt in millennial sects. Such groups are by definition an expression of elitism. They are sustained by a belief in their exclusive title to salvation. Waves of intolerance can radiate from the power of their convictions. At the same time, the very vehemence and unorthodoxy of their fervor can attract not only scorn, but also persecution.

An established religious hierarchy, millennial or not, has a vested interest in the retention or its emotional power. Frequently these bodies view any challenge to their belief systems either from outside, or within, as directly threatening to their control over the emotions of adherents. This threat, real or perceived, can become a vortex of intolerance, spewing accusation and punishment in all directions in the struggle for emotional power.

Similarly, a charismatic leader of a sect or group can regard any opposition to his or her authority as directly infringing upon emotional power. The response here can also be draconian. In both these cases the perpetuation of emotional power over a flock may not be an end in itself, that is likely to be salvation, but it is always a significant issue. The feelings surrounding this power are often so intense that they can easily burst into flame.

Mystics, holders of heterodox opinions, and others who might contest a hierarchy's claim for exclusive rights to absolute truth are often regarded as enemies of the status quo, as indeed they are. Those with vested interests in preserving emotional power can sometimes strike out verbally, psychologically or physically to retain their positions and influence. The result can be intolerance, discrimination, or persecution.

Geographical Power

The world is accustomed to the results of contests for geographic power. When the ingredient of religion is added to the mix the outcomes can be explosive. Attempts to control specific areas of geography have taken place throughout recorded history. Accompanying efforts to establish, extend control, or intensify belief systems has often deepened the complexities associated with geographic power. The form that these geo-religious contests assume could be an established faith battling a rising new entry for control over a given area.

The Catholic Church's efforts against the Cathari in thirteenth century southern France is one example. The Thirty Years' War (1687-1648), which was fought between Protestants and Catholics largely in Germany, was another. A struggle could develop between two adjacent states, or regions, each championing a different faith. The many clashes between Muslims and Christians, or Protestants and Catholics, are evidence of these rival bids for geographic power. The war between Shi'ite Iran and Sunni Iraq, both fighting for territory, was an interfaith version of geographical power struggle. A third instance can occur when an entity representing one belief system subdues an entity, or entities, adhering to a different belief or beliefs. The rule of Mughul India, which was Islamic, over its often rebellious Hindu (and other) subjects is an example of this situation. Finally, a religious minority in a given area can often serve as a lightening rod for like believers elsewhere to engage in efforts to "liberate" them or establish their independence. Currently Kashmir comes to mind, as does Nigeria.

Any, or all, of these conditions can lead to intolerance or worse. When control over a specific geographic area is at stake the intolerance can grow more severe. Discrimination can evolve into persecution, which can then grow into violence. Religion not only can deepen any contest over control over geography, it can also render these contests significantly more difficult to resolve, as the several crusades and the Islamic invasions of Europe attest. Regarding a geographical rival who has a different faith, the tendency to view with suspicion, alarm, or hatred is all the more pronounced. The Middle East and Northern Ireland have been continuing examples of this condition. Geography spiced by belief can be a lethal combination in the continual struggle over both persons and souls.

Economic Power

Economics, geography, and belief are closely related. Frequently they cannot be separated. But there is one constant: economic power causes fear, envy, and sometimes hatred, on the part of those who don't have it. Jews, Armenians, Sikhs, Alawites, Parsis and many others have been despised because of their economic prowess, which has been attributed by many to religion. As in other areas of power, these feelings can have many gradations, ranging from dislike to murderous rage. We see scenarios bearing such symptoms playing out every day all over the world.

In many cases the purity of belief provides a certain economic focus, and does enable strong connections to develop with fellow believers. Focus and connections often described as networks may be partly, or even wholly, responsible for economic accomplishment. Conditions prevailing in an area under the sway of a particular belief system, for example, the inability of Muslims around the world to charge interest may provide economic opportunity for members of another system such as Jews, Armenian Christians, or Parsis. When a certain group of believers succeed where rivals fail, or cannot go, resentment can follow, and expand.

This resentment can intensify at times of economic stress. It is human nature to blame someone else for one's own misfortune. If a larger, politically or religiously dominant group loses economic power to a smaller one unified by faith, the resentment is likely to develop into discrimination or persecution. Additionally, disadvantaged elements of any given society are prone to being the most resentful over the financial success that has eluded them. This is not unusual, but if resentment is honed when success accrues largely to the members of a single religious group it can attract lethal attention. The disadvantaged live at the margin and for them life is a zero sum game, with additions to any given group meaning subtractions from their own prospects. In these ways jealousy or resentment can be aroused by an incident, a charismatic leader, or a revival of old hatreds, and home in on the economic success of a particular group. If that group is ethically or religiously homogeneous, discrimination can be the result.

POLITICAL AUTHORITY

The several aspects involved with the attainment, retention, and expansion of political authority dovetail with the issues discussed in the previous section, especially with economic and geographic power. If religious overtones are mixed with political authority, the result can be a more cohesive social contract, or it may open canyons of divisiveness. Only individual particulars will be determinants, but whatever the situation vigilance to detect signs of change is important.[31]

The nature of a society's overtones can directly influence geopolitics and socio-economics, as they have in Israel, India, or Ireland. Hierarchies in both church and state can blend or compete; strengthen or enervate at many levels. The resultant interactions may produce stress or understanding, depending upon indigenous conditions as well as exogenous factors. If we comprehend the societal crosscurrents, then we can seek models of tolerance. If faith, especially if it is a different faith, is perceived to wield such economic control over certain people's lives then the ensuing resentment can erupt into flame at any moment. Should the presiding government be some sort of autocracy, it may frequently be in the interest of a presiding autocrat encourage this type of resentment in order to divert the focus of dissatisfaction from other causes. This behavior has produced pogroms and fueled religious wars. However, an even-handed economic policy can defuse political resentment, and this can be very important ingredient in any recipe for tolerance.

It can happen. The Emirate of Cordoba from the eighth to eleventh centuries under the Umayyad Islamic rule produced a remarkable example of a tolerant and vibrant society.[32] While we have become all too familiar with examples of vicious intolerance we do not expect tolerance from a fundamentalist theocracy. It can exist, and has. Asoka, ruler of the Buddhist Mauryan Empire in third century (BCE) Northern India, presided over one such state. William Penn's Quaker colony of Pennsylvania in the eighteenth century may be regarded as another. The Punjabi Sikh state of 1799 to 1849 was a model for theocratic democracy. There have been others illustrating that political authority tinted by religion does not have to be intolerant.

The Moghul[33] Emperor Akbar demonstrated during his long rule how fundamental beliefs (in this case Islam) do not need to be accompanied by active persecution and violence. In this he offered a dramatic contrast with his immediate Moghul Empire successors who were fervent and repressive Islamists.[34]

Akbar was born as his father Humayun (the second Moghul emperor, son of the Central Asian warlord Babur) was fleeing India for Persia in the wake of an assumption of power by an Afghan challenger. Humayun reestablished the Moghul Empire in 1555 when Akbar was twelve, but died one year later. Akbar defeated a number of contesters for his power, expanded the empire, and set up a capital at Fatehpur Sikiri, near Agra.

He was constantly searching for spiritual enlightenment and established a Muslim-like belief system with himself as center of worship. Despite this theocratic bent, Akbar lifted all discriminatory practices against Hindus, facilitated the formation of an extensive Sikh community, and welcomed representatives from India's many religions (including Portuguese Catholic priests from Goa) for extensive discussions on the nature of faith.

Akbar himself may have been the most powerful of Moghul rulers. But in the exercise of his power he demonstrated that strong political authority, even of a theocratic bent, does not require repression. Repression does create adverse reactions. Many of the world's great faiths have begun as reactions to overly domineering political or religious hierarchies. In their early years most of them have been nurtured by projecting a sense of egalitarianism. As religious hierarchies took hold this sense often faded into a more rigidly bureaucratic structure. At present we are confronted with examples of the disturbing nuances of Muslim theocracy in the Islamic Republic of Iran, in Saudi Arabia and in fragments of the recently demolished Taliban regime in Afghanistan. In other faiths repressive theocracies have arisen as well. Akbar tempered theocratic government by being open to discussions about different types of belief. His society tried to reduce the repressive weight of politico-religious hierarchy. It provides a useful example for study.

A book on the New Age practice of channeling made the following comment, which is broadly applicable. "From the perspective of people attracted to channeling and similar forms of improvisational spirituality, the major problem with formal religions is their alleged obsession with hierarchy and control."[35] When that obsession spills over into the political sector the combination has to be managed with great care lest it get out of hand.

All authority, whether vested in a social contract or religious covenant, requires some sort of submission.[36] Underlying and often straining against this submission is an egalitarian hope, attainable either in this life of some other. This hope can be expressed through an egalitarian political philosophy, or it can grow from inside religious belief. In rare cases, such as with the expressions of our Founding Fathers, there can be elements of both.

It may seem ironic to those of us faced with almost daily condemnations from extremist Muslims, but both religious fundamentalism and republican democracy attempt to shrink hierarchy and reinforce a concept of equality. A comprehensive guide for daily life may be imposed in the guise of religious practice, or it may assume the form of a constitutional document. In either case, it intends to represent the extension of power to wider swath of the population. In the religious case, the ultimate authority is vested in a divinity. Thus, fundamentalism of any faith is not inherently anti-democratic, although it can easily become so.

Hierarchies are usually imposed as supposedly necessary interlocutors for a less than informed polity. These too can be political or religious. Either way they are instruments of power. Even though they may purport to empower the powerless they tend to radiate the power of an elite cadre. But, as noted, fundamental religious cadres do not necessarily have to restrict egalitarian expression. Both fundamentalism and democracy, each in its own realm, can be allied as positive forces representing more benign authority. There is a delicate balance required of political authority, theocratic or not. Too little balance can promote chaos. Too much can result in repression. Historical examples of tolerance abound, and can serve as templates as long as intolerance does not creep in unannounced. Thus, the mixture of religious and political authority is not inherently combustible, but its control requires awareness, plus finely tuned technique.

ORDER

Authority's rationale is often order. Polities, lives, minds, and souls cry out for order. Chaos is considered anathema except for some, like Mao Tse Tung whose rule was based upon it. But for all its virtues, order can be a seductive concept. We all desire it – to a point. We will sacrifice to achieve it – to some degree. When exactly these points or degrees have been passed is a matter for continual debate. Those seeking to corral power may claim that is still distant. Those seeking to dissipate it will assert that it has long receded behind. The debate is perpetual, as is its connection to power through order. It enters our discussion because order is frequently constructed from the girders of belief.

To a significant extent order, whether it be personal, spiritual, or political, displaces uncertainty. Since uncertainty is an archenemy of inner peace, people are willing to make compromises so that it may be minimized. Many an authoritarian government, whether political or religious in nature, has been initially welcomed as a provider of order. The Taliban came to power in Afghanistan in that way, as did Idi Amin in Uganda. Only after these compromises have been proposed do the questions about extent begin. Only after compromises have been made can the order-created power incrementally move towards intolerance, be it political or religious.

Debate, dissent, and differences of belief can all threaten civil or interpersonal tranquility. However, restricting them in the interests of purported order can lead to repression. Finding an acceptable middle ground is the indispensable task of any functioning society. Our world is in the midst of an era when those skills, which can discover an appropriate middle ground, particularly in the area of belief, will increase in value. That value will be measured by the extent to which any given society can refrain from demonizing any of the systems or faiths expressed within its boundaries.

KNOWLEDGE

Francis Bacon proclaimed that "knowledge is power", a statement reaffirmed by the history of civilizations. Those with significant knowledge want to employ it, often to accumulate power. Some societies have been renown for exposing most of their citizens to knowledge. Others have been notorious for restricting knowledge to a small elite group. The struggle within societies over how to spread knowledge, or to determine who is entitled to it, is an important, even seminal one. No segment of knowledge is more important to or more controversial within any culture than the one involving belief. In most instances knowledge it is the ultimate source of power, and of exclusion.

Religious power is centered upon the divine conception and its transmission to believers. In most religions God has the knowledge, and simultaneously is the font for all knowledge. In monotheistic belief systems this power is further concentrated into one entity or concept. Consequently, those who claim knowledge of or about the divinity can control access to power. The important Islamic philosopher Abu Hamid Muhammad ibn Muhammad al-Ghazzali (1058-1111 CE) is one who advocated elitism, as was his posthumous rival Abu'-Walid Muhammad ibn Ahmad ibn Rushd (1126-1198 CE) who was known in Europe as Averroës. Both tried to limit the spread of available knowledge to a small group of the highly educated.

The type and structure of interlocutors for the divine vary from faith to faith. There are complex hierarchies. There are single gurus or adepts with informal authority. In most cases at least one person stands between the individual believer and the divinity, facilitating or interpreting. Some forms of mysticism are an exception, but they are relatively rare.

The interlocutors possess power derived from perceived divine knowledge. Sometimes power comes via the ability to effect a connection. Possessing the power of knowledge can either be benign or malignant. In its malignant form the power gained through knowledge is used both to control those within one's faith that do not possess it, and to repress those who believe differently.

I would amend Bacon to read, "knowledge is both power and danger." Under ideal circumstances it should be neither. Knowledge should be the property of all, given in large enough dollops to spread the power of belief evenly, and thus feared by none. Regretfully, circumstances are only rarely and briefly ideal. Consequently, the potential for intolerance born from restricted knowledge looms all too large.

LOVE

There are many kinds of love. All of them in one way or another have been used to express and describe emotions human beings devote to some divinity. As all of us realize, emotions rising out of devotion are not always rational or reasonable. Love generated by religious belief is likely to be a site for particularly intense feeling. This should come as no surprise since religious love, of any variety, stems from deep conviction. It wells up from an individual's innermost resources carrying with it the purest and most fervid emotions. These can be employed for good or for ill. Their deeply personal nature makes these feelings unpredictable, and at times impenetrable.

Love for a divinity who provides "the answer" is profound, and usually admirable. It can foster a vision of a path wide and compassionate enough to accommodate all, regardless of their status or orientation. It can inspire missionary zeal, which balances precariously upon the line between tolerance and its obverse. It can also ignite hatred and repression, fueled by the jealousy or an insecure proprietor. The variety of possibilities, which can change with apparent randomness, may make love at once the most valuable and the most dangerous characteristic of all, especially when it is applied to belief.

CODA

In this chapter we have seen that many motivations for religious belief, and action on behalf of belief, exist. Some of these beliefs and actions can spawn intolerance for those who do not believe and act similarly. We have also seen that most of these motivations can be differently employed to encourage tolerance. And that is our societal challenge. Can we keep these visceral emotions from boiling over? Or will we allow ourselves to slip into the abyss of religious prejudice? The results may well determine the way the American version of Western civilization will be categorized. But in all cases tolerance must be accompanied by a willingness to comprehend the belief systems of others, regardless of whether we agree with them or not. Before we touch upon some of the potential outcomes for the coming century, we need to take a brief look at the societal damage resulting from bursts of intolerance.

---

[1] For more on this subject and its implications see: John Seer, *Political Theory for Mortals: Shades of Justice, Images of Death* (Ithaca: Cornell University Press, 1996); Ernest Becker, *The Denial of Death* (New York: The Free Press, 1973); Robert Pogue Harrison, *The Dominion of the Dead* (Chicago: University of Chicago Press, 2004); and

Timothy Taylor, *The Buried Soul: How Humans Invented Death* (Boston: Beacon Press, 2002).

[2] Stephen Alter, *Sacred Waters*, (New York: Harcourt, Inc, 2001), p. 239.

[3] Nils Ahnlund, *Gustavus Adolphus the Great*, translated by Michael Roberts (New York: History Book Club, 1999), p. 128.

[4] Wade Davis, *The Serpent and the Rainbow*, (New York: Simon and Schuster, 1995) p. 217. Davis was writing about the voodoo society of Haiti.

[5] Orlando Figes, *Natasha's Dance: A Cultural History of Russia* (New York: Metropolitan Books, 2002) p. 345 – A further discussion goes on until p. 354.

[6] Stephen E. Ambrose, *Band of Brothers*, (Simon & Schuster, 1992) p. 140-141.

[7] One of the more poignant analyses of approaching death was recounted by Harvard Medical School's Dr. Jerome Groopman in a Parade magazine article containing excerpts from his new book: *The Anatomy of Hope: How People Prevail in the Face of Illness*, (Random House).

> Are you afraid I asked? Her months of candor had encouraged mine. 'You know, not really, not as much as I thought I might be.' I moved my chair closer to hers. 'Why do you think that is?' I'm not entirely sure. I have strange comforting thoughts.' She shifted onto her side so she could face me. 'When fear starts to creep up on me, I conjure the idea that millions and millions of people have passed away before me, and millions more will pass after I do. Then I think: My parents each died. I guess if they all did it, so can I.' She paused. 'As Ecclesiastes says, everything has its season – a time to be born and a time to die. And as a Christian, I believe in a hereafter, that we can return to God. What form that takes no one can really say.' Barbara grinned. 'It's not like I'm expecting to get on the Up escalator and be delivered to paradise. Or find Angels there playing harps. I was never one for airy music. I want to believe in an afterlife, but sometimes it's hard to imagine." I said. Barbara's tone turned grave. 'Of course I also have doubts. Everyone who believes has doubt if they're honest with themselves. I suppose it could all be an illusion. But deep inside, it doesn't feel that way at all.

[8] Leon R. Kass, MD, *Life Liberty and the Defense of Dignity*, (San Francisco: Encounter Books, 2002) p. 48.

[9] Carlos Casteñeda, *The Teachings of Don Juan* (Berkeley: University of California Press, reprinted in 1998) author's commentary.

[10] Keith Ward, *Religion and Community* (Oxford: Clarendon Press, 2000) p. 135.

[11] Pierre Teilhard de Chardin, *Activation of Energy*, tr. By René Hague (New York: Harcourt, Brace Javanovich, 1979) p. 400.

[12] Ernest Becker, *The Denial of Death*, (New York: The Free Press, 1973) p 203.

[13] Isaiah 6:5.

[14] Václav Havel, The Power of the Powerless" in *Open Letters*, selected and edited by Paul Wilson (New York: Vintage Books, 1992) p. 129.

[15] For more on this subject see: Pierre Teilhard de Chardin, *Activation of Energy*, translated by René Hague, (New York: Harcourt Brace Jovanovich, 1963).

[16] For a discussion of the atheistically scientific-belief conflict see: Kenneth R. Miller, *Finding Darwin's God*, (Cliff Street Books 1999).

[17] For a comprehensive discussion of atheism see: Michael Moutin, *Atheism: A Philosophical Justification*, (Temple University Press, 1990).

[18] Joshua 24:14-15. Another example can be seen in Amos 3:12, as he warns the people of Israel, "You only have I known of all the families of the earth; therefore I will punish

you for your iniquities." My attention to these statements was drawn from Karen Armstrong in *A History of God*, (Alfred A. Knopf).

[19] Stephen Alter in *Sacred Waters*, (New York: Harcourt Inc., 2000) at p. 120, outlines a similar fear: "Through the Brahmin priests of Kharsali (near one of the four Himalayan sources of the Ganges) attend to the worship of Yamuna Devi (the river goddess), the largest temple in their village is dedicated to Shani Devta, god of the planet Saturn. He is known throughout India as a dark and unpredictable deity. Astrologers warn that if a man is born under the inauspicious sign of Saturn he will endure continuous suffering and misfortune. For this reason Shani is worshipped more our of fear than devotion."

[20] For more on this subject see: James L. Kugel, *The God of Old: Inside the World of the Bible*, (New York: The Free Press, 2003).

[21] Karen Armstrong, *A History of God*, (Alfred A. Knopf 1993) p 130.

[22] Edmondo Lupieri, *The Mandaeans: The Last Gnostics*, tr. By Charles Hindley, (Grand Rapids, MI: William B. Eerdman's Publishing Co., 2002), p. 32.

[23] Ibid, pages 247-250 describe this phenomenon.

> According to the Mandaeans, Jesus, after his ignominious death, returns to his heaven (Mercury's) where, given that he is a demonical reality, he carries out his allotted task of guarding the house of punishment (*matarta*) entrusted to him. ...The soul of the Mandaean having left the body rises from *matarta* to *matarta*. As soon as it sees each one, it is seized with terror, invokes the Life, is answered, shows the guardians its name and marks of its Mandaean faith (baptism, radiance...), and is left free to continue to rise.

[24] See *Showings*, James Walsh, ed. (Paulist, 1978) for a medieval story of compassion and love involving the female mystical recluse, Julian of Norwich (1342-1412), who wrote *Revelations of Divine Love*.

[25] These rules, drawn up in the monastery of Monte Cassino called for a conversion of fear to love. This transformation was to be achieved through strict discipline administered by a central authority.

[26] For a description of what can happen to the priesthood when the rains fail see Jared Diamond's *Collapse* (New York: Viking, 2005) and his description of the Anasazi.

[27] Walter Burkert, in his renowned *Greek Religion* (Cambridge, MA: Harvard University Press, 1985), describes what happened to the Pythagorean colony in the mid-fifth century BCE The ascetic Pythagoreans, who lived in a settlement in Corona, Sicily, had a belief system heavily overlain with Eastern influences, including some from the teachings of Buddha who was Pythagoras' contemporary. Their system featured a doctrine of meteonpsychosis or reincarnation. His colony was burnt and many inhabitants massacred. Burkert elaborates: "Civil war was no rarity in Greek cities; yet here for the first time it seems to have led to a kind of pogrom, the persecution of those who were different from others in their way of life and disposition."

[28] Maria Rosa Menocal, *The Ornament of the World: How Muslims, Jews, and Christians Created a Culture of Tolerance in Medieval Spain*, (Boston: Little Brown and Company, 2002), p. 11.

[29] For an intriguing analysis of how religious beliefs affect the accumulation of wealth (belief in hell increases economic growth) see: Robert Barrows and Rachael McCleary in the Spring 2004 issue of *American Sociological Review*.

[30] This can be summed up in one sentence from page 35 of Edmond Lupieri's book (translated by Charles Hindley), The *Mandaeans*, published by William B. Eerdmaris in 2002. "Ears to hear and eyes to see, this is the tragic ability of the Gnostic." They believe they can discern the true word of God and at the same time can perceive the level of hatred directed against them.

[31] The increasing overlap between church and state in Christian and Muslim settings, for example, has solicited, as one might expect, both positive and negative response. Father Richard John Neuhaus, a Roman Catholic priest and the editor of *First Things*, the philosopher Michael Novak, and Professor Hugh Heclo each have applauded this development, contrarily secular humanist Paul Kurtz and author Wendy Kaminar are cautiously apprehensive.

[32] For more on this subject see Maria Rosa Menocal, *The Ornament of the World*, (New York: Little Brown and Co., 2002).

[33] There are various spellings of this word including: Mughal, Mogul and Moghul. I have selected the latter for the Central Asian Islamic dynasty that ruled India from 1526 until the British conquest.

[34] Akbar ruled from 1542 to 1605. He was succeeded by his son Jahangir (1605-1627), later by and his grandson Shah Jihan (1621-1658), builder of the Taj Mahal.

[35] Michael Brown, *The Channeling Zone*, (Harvard University Press, 1997), p. 117.

[36] For example, the word *Islam* in Arabic means "submission".

Chapter Three

Societal Damage

As for heretics, their sin deserves banishment, not only from the Church by
excommunication, but also from the world by death.[1]

Saint Thomas Aquinas (1225-1274)

Millions have died in theological ideological, nationalistic, political, and
racial conflicts spread throughout the twentieth century. In some areas they still
continue. These tragedies have occurred most infamously in Northern Ireland,
between India and Pakistan, against the Armenians after World War I, with the
Holocaust, and the perpetual fulmination of hatred in the Middle East. There are
perhaps a dozen other similar examples of conflict with horrific consequences
that could be gleaned from the reports ricocheting around today's world. In this
chapter we will dig a bit deeper to discern overt and covert societal damage
emanating from several varieties of religious intolerance. One factor is a
constant; whenever intolerance surfaces in whatever form, there are
repercussions adversely affecting human beings. The more virulent the
expressions of intolerance are, the greater the damage. As stimulating as Saint
Thomas might have been for Catholic theology, and as great was his moral
influence, the attitude expressed in this chapter's opening quote can have a
ruinous impact upon any society to which it is applied.

COLLISIONS

The most dramatic societal damage reverberates when opposing belief systems collide – politically, ideologically, or militarily. The field of battle, be it a page, a pulpit, or a swath of territory, can undergo a degree of conflict beyond mere intellectual sparring. When this occurs tempers flare, rhetoric soars, swords are drawn and confrontation is direct. To get to this point views had to have been narrowed, reason had to have departed (or be well on its way out the door), and the gates of receptivity had to have been shut.

Protestants and Catholics in many locations throughout history have endured collisions. Few have been as far ranging and as destructive as the Thirty Years' War in Europe (1618-1648). India and Pakistan, pitting Hindus against Muslim, are a modern example of prolonged religious collision, which extends within and across national borders. For centuries the various disciplines of Islam, often collected into distinct political entities, have campaigned against one another in a number of ways. The several crusades of the Middle Ages (by Christians against both Muslims and heretics, as well as by Muslims as jihads against both unbelievers and heretics.) were particularly bloody.[2] Between 1096 and 1291 there were nine crusades undertaken by Europeans against Middle Eastern Muslims. In addition there were approximately ten more prior to 1500 waged by Europeans against pagans and presumed heretics in Germany, France, Central Europe and the Balkans. In most cases they were intolerant clashes with socio-economic overtones that persisted for decades, even centuries.

Virtually every faith and every nation (or empire) has endured, or undertaken, at one time or another a substantial and violent collision over differing religious or economic beliefs. During the thousands of years of recorded history these collisions have resulted in tens of millions being killed and many times that number being injured. If we inspect each of these episodes to learn why it happened, what it cost society, and whether it could have been prevented, we might carry some useful lessons into the future. One such example is the crusade by the established Catholic church against the sect in southern France called Cathari, or Albigensians.

This crusade contains elements of the motivations discussed in the previous chapter, retention of geographical, organizational, and emotional power. Descended from Gnostic and Docetic[3] beliefs, the Cathari were related to the Manichaeans of the Near East and the Bogomils of the Balkans. In the twelfth century the sect emerged in southern France. The believers' home was a remote mountainous region adjacent to the Pyrenees, and centered on the town of Albi. The people of the region spoke Occitan, or Provençal, which provided the area's name (Lange 'd 'oc, or Languedoc, which means "the language of Oc"). The major Catharis/Albigensian fortified strong point was Carcasonne, and the seat of local government was Toulouse.

The Cathari (derived from the Greek word for "pure ones") followed an ascetic form of religion which rejected both the sacraments and the church hierarchy, considered the Bible an allegory, and taught that Jesus only appeared to take human form but was never actually a human being. Their universe was dualistic (Manichaean), being divided into the realms of God and the Evil One. Their leaders, or Perfects, were strict observers of an extremely ascetic ritual who interpreted the faith for the majority. Similar to the Docetists, Cathari considered the flesh alien to the spirit. Strict dietary laws that eliminated anything related to flesh (including milk) were observed, especially among the Perfects. Meals were ritually prepared and eaten. Celibacy was popular, notably by Perfects, as was extreme mortification of human flesh, often taking the form of suicide by starvation.

Due to the exemplary lives of their Perfects, compared to the corruption that was perceived to exist within the hierarchy of both the church and the secular government, the Cathari began to gain followers in the mid-to late twelfth century. Consequently, the established church grew concerned. Its control over the region was slipping. Its power base in France, Spain, and northern Italy seemed threatened. At first the great Cistercian, Bernard of Clairveaux, and some of his monks arrived by papal request (in 1167) to preach and pray in the mountain villages and towns in order to peacefully restore Catholic hegemony. This effort was not successful. Neither was a subsequent effort by the Dominicans. In 1209 Pope Innocent III proclaimed a crusade against the Cathari faithful. The crusade's leader was the great and ruthless French noble with English connections, Simon de Montfort (1160-1218). He was Count of Montfort by his father, and was Earl of Leicester by his mother. Montfort was a veteran of the Fourth Crusade (1202-1204) and was an intensely religious man. He was ambitious, coveting the lands of Raymond VI Count of Toulouse and King Pedro II of Aragon, the Cathari's principal supporters. Backed by the papal declaration, Simon's army invaded Languedoc. He took Carcasonne in 1209, Toulouse in 1215, and decisively defeated the combined forces of Raymond and Pedro. The region was ransacked and Simon was made Viscount of Béziers and Carcasonne by his army. The stage was set for peace when he died in 1218. The Treaty of Paris eventually concluded a very tenuous peace in 1229.

Although Simon's victory had been decisive, it was not complete. Even military losses, looting and repression did not deter the hardy mountaineers from following their faith in secret. They were guided, as before, by Perfects who wended their way at night from village to village along obscure mountain paths. Innocent's nephew Pope Gregory IX was outraged at this persistence, and established the monastic Inquisition in 1233. Dominican Inquisitors were assigned to root out the heresy.

Over the next one hundred years conversions, inquests, executions, their own celibacy, and suicide caused the Cathari to be greatly reduced in number. The economy of the region suffered. Society was laced with mistrust. Many died for their beliefs. Even today the remote mountain villages of Languedoc are only tangentially a part of France, and remain suspiciously insular.[4]

Another form of collision, with which Americans have become disturbingly familiar recently, is terrorism with a religious component. A wedge of religiously tainted violence, whether from terror, warfare, or persecution, can disrupt economic and intellectual commerce. Inhabitants of Sri Lanka, Kashmir and the Palestinian sectors of Israel have learned this lesson, much to their dismay. In Central Africa religion and ethnicity can be intertwined. When disputes arise thy can ignite society-rending violence. Persecutions of Christians and Muslims in China have had economic and psychological implications, as well as physical ones. Iranian youths charging unarmed against Iraqi fortifications in the 1981 to 1989 war or suicide bombers detonating themselves may be seeking an ethereal reward, which inspired their deadly and apparently irrational actions. Those orchestrating violent incidents or a religious nature may have as their purpose the promotion of a particular view through threat or denial.[5]

Religious violence can take on varied forms. In the latter portion of his life Saint Augustine became convinced that unbelievers, schismatics, and heretics could be brought into the fold of orthodox Christianity by force. He translated a quotation of Jesus (reciting the parable of the banquet) to read: "compel those outside to come in."[6] This translation laid the foundation for a practice of forced conversions, and ultimately for the theological reasoning behind the Inquisition and the Crusades. Whether Saint Augustine himself would have sanctioned these violent extensions of his interpretation is problematical. In fact, his relative tolerance in a deeply unsettled age was noteworthy. However, violence occurred, and he was cited as one source for its justification.

By the time of the beginning of the Reformation[7], violent attacks on heretics, tortuous inquisitions and forced conversions had become infamous practices. Both the Catholic Church and the new Protestants did not hesitate to persecute those with alternate beliefs. John Calvin's Protestant Geneva was a cruel and austere city no less oppressive than those dominated by Catholic inquisitors. Given the prevalent religious tension, it was no surprise when what seemed like all of Europe chose sides for a war over faith. That war, which became known as the Thirty Years War, first erupted in 1618, when several Protestant churches were closed and destroyed in Bohemia by the minions of the Holy Roman Emperor Mathias I (1557-1619).

Protestant rebels led by Count Matthias von Turn invaded the palace in Prague and threw two imperial envoys from one of the windows. (Although they fell 50 feet, they survived.) In the ensuing war the Protestant Union of Frederick IV, who was Elector Palatine, fought the German Catholic League, which was nominally headed by the Holy Roman Emperor.[8] Initially the Catholic armies prevailed, led by the brilliant Bavarian marshal Johannes Tserclaes, Count of Tilly (who historians today usually refer to by name as Tilly). By 1630 the tide turned as the Swedish king, and great military commander, Gustavus Adolphus (1594-1632) entered the fray.[9]

Over the first third of the seventeenth century the war decimated Central Europe, and involved much of the rest of Europe in the contest. It culminated in the Treaty of Westphalia (October 24, 1648), which ushered in the era of nation-states. Hundreds of thousands were killed, wounded, and displaced. Much of Europe's economy was shredded. The battle lines of religious antipathy were imbedded, and to some extent these hostilities are still reflected in Europe's geopolitics.

REPRESSIONS

Religious intolerance in the form of repression can surface in a number of forms. Each form includes targeting an oppositional religious belief system, and seeking to then minimize or even remove it. Depending upon the degree of alarm or hostility fueling the repression against those being, or to be, repressed, has as its object the minimization, rooting out, and/or removal from the theological or sociological mainstream. The methods used to expose and exorcise the oppositional religious belief systems may become insidiously merciless.

Pope Gregory IX (1227-1241) established the Inquisition in 1232, following the Holy Roman Emperor Frederick II's (1220-1250) urging, to hunt down heretics. The immediate cause, as noted above, was the proliferation of the Cathari in southern France. The Dominicans and Franciscans were put in charge of conducting the inquiries. Pope Innocent IV (1243-1254). Twenty years later, in 1252, torture was authorized by a bull from Pope Innocent IV (1243-1254). The separate and even more feared Spanish Inquisition was established by Pope Sixtus IV (1471-1484) in 1478, and originally designed to uncover insincere converts to Christianity from Judaism and Islam. As the reconquest of Spain from the Muslims by Ferdinand and Isabella was concluded in 1492, many Jews and Muslims converted to Christianity to avoid fines, discrimination, and expulsion. Suspicion concerning converts and their descendents persisted for centuries, accompanying efforts to "purify the faith".

Catholics have been persecuted in various ways in scattered locations over the entire range of their existence. In the earliest days of Christianity Romans, Jews and others engaged in repression. In the Middle Ages there were Muslim *jihads* directed against Christians. In the nineteenth and twentieth centuries United States Catholics, especially newly arrived immigrants experienced both active and passive discrimination or repression. Buddhists, Hindus, and virtually every other faith have been on the receiving end of discriminatory or repressive practices. Apparently, these activities play a strong role in the makeup of human nature. Could this stem from fundamental insecurity? Regardless of the source, repression, discrimination, and persecution always cause societal damage.

What is to be done when a particular practice, or series of practices, falls outside the boundaries of a valid social contract? Obviously, human sacrifice would be considered murder in most countries. Smoking marijuana, polygamy, and use of hallucinogenic substances, to cite three examples, are all considered valid practices with religious undertones in some areas but not in others. (The United States prohibits them.) Is prosecution under existing laws persecution? Some might answer that it is, but enforcement of a valid legal code is not inherently repressive, although the intentions behind the code's original enactment might be. However, more extreme measures that stretch or exceed the legal code might well be repressive in nature.

The Nazi extermination and incarceration of Jews and the Stalinist Soviet Union's persecution of Russian Orthodox believers were carried out with at least tangential legal justification. They were violent repressions nonetheless. Conversely, societies that legally support toleration but allow or even encourage discrimination, which can turn lethal, are no less morally culpable. It is evident that lines drawn in this area applicable to religious belief can be indistinct or open to debate. While there may at times be an acceptable justification for some form of discrimination, if that means refusal to sanction all practices claimed to be religious, there is little excuse for repression if that means persecution.

A form of repression that falls into a category not always violent is restriction or stigmatization directed against a particular group because of its beliefs. This repression is apt to focus upon an easily identifiable group. Identification can be through dress, skin color, or ritual. The rationale behind these forms of repression theologically arises from a viewpoint that God himself differentiates between the favored and the non-favored. Wherever there is religious repression of any kind, believers who count themselves as members of the repressed belief system may suffer physical or emotional degradation simply because of what they believe.

Reflection upon how these attitudes of fear, distrust, and hatred become ingrained as well as dangerous to a society might limit the potential damage. A recent study of Northern Ireland children conducted by the University of Ulster uncovered some disturbing facts.[10] The study followed 352 children aged 3 to 6 who were drawn equally from Protestant and Catholic households. It found that a pattern of prejudice was instilled in them as early as the age of 3. Unprompted derogatory comments emerged from the children due to the intense hatreds that had been developed. This study, similar to one in 1999, which focused on the attitudes of Israeli and Palestinian children, revealed that such a foundation of intolerance could easily flare into acts of violence. If society is to be spared excessive damage, conscious efforts need to be made to decipher the bases of others' beliefs.

Repression, even in its most violent forms, can come from those who are supposed to be the society's holiest members. In the Islamic Republic of Iran Shi'ite clerics have instituted regulations in accordance with their interpretation of the Qu'ran. These regulations have been particularly onerous for women, in that repressive rules seek to curtail their intellectual, professional, and societal development. A female professor of literature writes about her observations and their affect on young women who were her students in Teheran.

> Their dilemmas, regardless of their backgrounds and beliefs, were shared, and stemmed from the confiscation of their most intimate moments and private aspirations by the regime. This conflict lay at the heart of the paradox created by Islamic rule. Now that the mullahs ruled the land, religion was used as an instrument of power, an ideology. It was this ideological approach to faith that differentiated those in power from millions of ordinary citizens.[11]

This is by no means a unique example, either historically or presently. Similar actions have taken place elsewhere in Islam, in Christianity, in Judaism, in Hinduism, in Buddhism, and in many other faiths over the centuries.

South Asia has experienced many repressions due to religious beliefs. Hindu-Muslim strife has plagued the Indian subcontinent since the arrival of the Moghuls under Babur in 1526. In the last few years some of the worst clashes have occurred in Gujarat. It was December of 1992 when an aroused Hindu mob demolished a sixteenth century mosque, the Babi Masjid, which they claimed had been built over the birthplace of their god Rama. Since that time many of the most violent depredations have been organized and carried out by militant Sadhus, who are itinerant Hindu ascetics widely considered to be holy. Sadhus have often been inspired by Ramchandra Paramhaus[12], whose appearance is akin to that of a non-age specific Santa Claus. The flames of imbedded hatreds, fanned by Paramhaus and his Sadhus, have scorched tens of thousands. Many Gujarafi Muslims have been killed along with a lesser number of Hindus, and many more have been terrorized by mobs spewing hate. The economy of this peninsula state northwest of Mumbai (Bombay) teeters as its people bleed from religious fury, and commerce grinds to a halt.

As Zen Buddhist priest and historian, Brian Victoria, points out in his two books, *Zen at War*[13] (1997) and *Zen War Stories*[14] (2002), this usually pacifistic Buddhist belief expression has played an important role in Japanese military culture dating back to the medieval days of the Samurai. Religious tenets infused martial thought and action, using the principles of this normally gentle and meditative form of Buddhism.

Theological debate about the nature and means of "salvation" should never be the point of instigation for social prejudice, discrimination, or repression. Within most societies it is not considered harmful or improper simply to have belief systems whose tenets hold that members of other belief systems will not attain salvation. Similarly, most societies accept attempts by members of specific belief systems to proselytize through non-coercive reasoned dialogue those who hold different beliefs. However, when members of a particular belief system are subjected to prejudice, discrimination, and repression because of their faith, society as a whole suffers.

EXACTIONS

It is not unusual for religiously influenced governments, or theocracies, to impose constraints upon individuals or groups that do not worship as they dictate. Taxation has been one such method of exaction. For example, although often tolerant of "people of the book" (i.e., Jews and Christians), Muslim governments often have imposed special taxes upon all non-Muslims. Laws requiring certain people to wear specific types of clothing, so as to make identification of them conspicuous, was a method of religious-based discrimination in some medieval jurisdictions, as well as in Nazi Germany. In some cases nations such as in the reign of Edward I (1272-1307) and Spain after 1492, resorted to expulsion for religious and economic reasons. In these two instances the victims were Jews. In 1948 millions of Muslims were removed from India to help form Pakistan (millions more remained). More recently, religious-based ethnicity has caused large-scale population displacements.

Bosnia, where Muslims, Croats, (Catholics) and Serbs (Russian Orthodox) were uprooted from their homes is but one example.

Laws denying rights or opportunities, or imposing monetary penalties upon certain religious groups, exist in various societies to this day. These can define status. They can channel people into particular occupations. They can deprive residents of political representation, or even of a say in the process of societal formation. It should be intuitively obvious that few if any of these measures are of long run benefit to the underlying polity.

A PAINFUL EXAMPLE

Dollars and cents are only one way of measuring what virulent faith-based intolerance costs any society. Loss of trade, retarded economic development, myopic political systems, loss of income from tourism, and increased military expenses are a few of these direct ramifications. Sri Lanka, for one, suffers from all these types of penalties.[15]

As it emerged from colonialism Sri Lanka (then called Ceylon) looked a fair bet to flourish. It had an industrial base. It had an educated elite. Because of its pleasing climate and natural beauty it had a thriving tourism industry.

On February 4, 1948 the British Crown Colony of Ceylon became a self-governing dominion. In 1954 a congress of Buddhist monks, educators and lay people published a report, "Betrayal of Buddhism," It was a militantly religious and nationalistic protest against both colonial rule and its immediate successor. In 1956 Sinhala was declared the official language. The Sinhalese majority instituted policies that severely penalized Tamil who were located mostly in the island's northwest quadrant. These lone ago immigrants from southern India had their educational and commercial opportunities restricted. The Tamil minority (25%) rioted over these policies. They began calling for either devolution of power or the creation of a separate Tamil state (Eelam).

In 1972 Ceylon proclaimed itself the Republic of Sri Lanka (the Sinhalese name for the island). In so doing the majority reaffirmed its belief that a Buddhist theocracy was necessary. "The cause of preserving Sri Lanka as a sovereign undivided Sinhala Buddhist state is so paramount that the main body of the Sangha has not felt the moral imperative to object to the tribulations imposed on Tamil civilians."[16] These tribulations included anti-Tamil riots, often led by monks, which occurred in 1977, 1981, and 1983. The army (virtually all Sinhalese) was sent out to repress the Tamils.

The Sinhalese are Theravada Buddhists.[17] There are 14 million Theravadas, 3.4 million Tamils, and 1.3 million Muslims in Sri Lanka. The Tamils are Hindus. They are descended from those who invaded in the 4th to 5th centuries CE from a region of southern India now called Tamil Nadu.

The Federal Party of the Tamils was outlawed in 1961. By 1986 the Liberation Tigers of Tamil Eelam were in full rebellion supported by co-religionists in Southern India. The Tigers developed the tactic of suicide bombing well before it surfaced in the Middle East. Far more suicide bombers from the Tamil rebels have blown themselves up in Sri Lanka than have

Palestinians in Israel. Over the years approximately 65,000 people have been killed and 1.6 million displaced by the conflict, which has spread throughout the island, although being most intense in the Tamil northeast.

The process of rebellion and terror by the Tamils resulted in attacks on Buddhist shrines and civilians. The Indian army (55,000 strong) was called in to maintain the peace in 1987, but failed to do so and subsequently left. Neither the passage of the Prevention of Terrorism Act (1979), nor the arming of Sinhalese citizens worked. The Buddhist right consisting of the monk-led Mabina Surakime Vyaparaya, and the even more militant Janatha Vikmathic Peramana, hardened. All settlement attempts evaporated in the face of terror and repression. After decades of fighting some recent measures appear to have made limited progress, and peace may be in sight.

Today Sri Lanka is at the bottom of most world economic indexes (e.g. economic freedom, inflation rate, quality of life, foreign debt, unemployment). Its defense spending as a percentage of gross domestic product (GDP) is one of the highest (5.1%). Other problems include early marriages, depleted forests, crowded roads, low life expectancy, and minimal spending on health (3.1% of GDP). But there is a ray of hope. A 2002 cease-fire seems to be holding reasonably well, as the exhausted combatants regroup and figure how to repair their shattered economies. Negotiations, leading toward a federation with regional Tamil autonomy in the northeast are proceeding and may yet yield a viable outcome that can serve as a foundation for future recovery.

Religious conflict (spilling over into nationalism and socioeconomic repression) has decimated a once promising country. Its past is fiery; its present is precarious; its future is cloudy. Intolerance and its ramifications have shredded its Sri Lankan prospects. Perhaps the first shaky step toward restoration has just been taken, but they are coming from depths not foreseen in the first post-colonial days of 1948.

THE OBVERSE

Any analysis of the burdens of social upheaval must also include consideration of possible or actual benefits. The story of medieval Andalusia, which later would become Spain, Portugal, and Andorra, is one of movement from repression, to a flowering tolerance, then back to repression. When Abd al-Rahman arrived in Cordoba in 755 CE to keep alive the Umayyad dynasty (which had been shorn of its Caliphate in Damascus five years earlier), he brought to fruition an odd but effective combination of Christians and Sephardic Jews under Muslim rule. His dynasty lasted for almost three hundred years. Those years constituted a high water mark for religious tolerance in Europe.[18]

First under Abd al-Rahman, then under his successors, the Umayyad Emirate was a multi-cultural, multi-ethnic, multi-religious blend that included Muslims, Christians, and Jews. This blend succeeded the Visigoths, who had arrived from the North in the early eighth century and had preserved a vaguely Roman (Latin speaking) Arian version of Christianity.[19] The Visigoths had not been especially tolerant. However, they were mild rulers compared to the Muslim puritans from

North Africa who eventually succeeded the Umayyads, and the Spain created by Ferdinand and Isabella in 1992.

Abd al-Rahman displaced some local Muslim and a few Christian warlords, loosely uniting the peninsular kingdom around his capital at Cordoba. The centuries of Umayyad rule were ones of economic, political and social integration. They were years of culture and scholarship, in which the works of Greek classical philosophers were translated into Arabic. Libraries were built on a grand scale. Cordoba's largest library had one thousand times as many books as the largest monastic library in Christian Europe, and was considered as second only to the great library in Alexandria. Sciences flourished, as did art, with mathematics and medicine being specialties.

As Umayyad rule began to break down by the mid-eleventh century, Muslim puritans represented by the Almoravid dynasty, invaded across the straits of Gibralter from present-day Morocco. They even brought religious intolerance in their wake. By the early twelfth century the more viciously puritan Almohads, also from North Africa, had assumed power. They held this sway over the peninsula for nearly a century. Their collectively repressive ways, reinforced by those of their Christian successors, decimated the culture and harmony that had marked the Umayyad years. It took hundreds of years for the Iberian Peninsula to recover. Even so, on a relative basis, it has never exceeded the dazzling ecumenical accomplishments of the Umayyad centuries.

A very similar pattern was traced in Baghdad from the ninth to the thirteenth centuries. As the capital of the Islamic Abbasid Caliphate[20], the city was a center of accomplishment. Scientific development, philosophical writing, poetry, architecture, medicine, literature, mathematics, and trade all flourished. Indeed, Baghdadis such as Omar Khayyam, Abu Hamid al-Ghazali, Ibn Sina (known also as Avicenna), Ibn Khaldun, Abu Al-Nasr al-Farabi, Muhammed ibn Musa al-Khwarismi, Alhazer, and dozens of other Muslim intellectuals were leading figures around the world. Numerous religions and cultures could be found on Baghdad's busy streets. Prosperity abounded. But then all of this changed. The Mongols sacked the city in 1258, and a succession of strict religionists of revolving ethnicity controlled this once cosmopolitan region. As the focus of ecumenical and vital Islam shifted west to the Ottomans and east to the Shi'ite Savafids, Baghdad slid into disrepair and a cultural obscurity from which it has never recovered.

SOME RECENT STATEMENTS OF RELIGIOUS INTOLERANCE

There are indeed detrimental societal costs that flow from religious intolerance. History is replete with examples of it, and of its obverse. Destructive repression is more than merely unjust because it robs civilization of the creative interaction, which is its lifeblood. Contrarily, tolerance can foster a climate of productive creativity.

Currently, the world includes some areas where religious intolerance has taken a heavy toll. Northern Ireland, the Balkans, the Middle East, and West Africa are examples.

There are also areas in which a few wisps of flame may portend a wider conflagration. Representative incidents were reported in the media during October of 2003. By themselves they may not be significant, or they may be harbingers.

Retiring Malaysian Prime Minister Mahathin gave a speech to the Organization of the Islamic Conference that met in Putrajaya, Malaysia.[21] In that speech he complained of Western persecution against Islam: "Today we, the whole Muslim ummah, are treated with contempt and dishonor. Our religion is denigrated, our holy places desecrated. Our countries are occupied, our people starved and killed."[22] Then he moved to gratuitously inflammatory language in placing ultimate blame for this persecution: "The Jews rule the world by proxy. They get others to fight and die for them."[23]

That same month it was revealed that Lt. Gen. William E. "Jerry" Boykin, an active duty United States Army general currently serving as deputy undersecretary of defense for intelligence, had made a number of appearances in uniform before Evangelical Christian audiences.[24] At those meetings he told the listeners that the United States was a "Christian nation" joined in "spiritual battle" against Satan.[25] He referred to a certain Somali Muslim leader by saying, "I knew that my God was bigger that his God. I knew that my God was a real God, and his was an idol."[26] These and other aspects of General Boykin's personal experiences or of his religious beliefs may not by themselves do more than to stir up a particular audience. However, when a senior officer while in uniform serving as a high Defense Department official gives them such blunt inflammatory language, they lend credibility to religious intolerance and step across the line separating church and state.

About a year earlier some evangelical pastors, specifically Franklin Graham, Jerry Falwell and Jerry Vines, all of the Southern Baptist Convention, made derogatory remarks about Islam generally and the Prophet Mohammed specifically. (The National Association of Evangelicals later denounced their personal attack on Mohammed as "dangerous" and "unhelpful".) Perhaps these attacks were envisioned as a bit of "turn-about is fair play." Wahhabi clerics in Saudi Arabia and elsewhere have long been demonizing Christians especially Americans in the harshest terms.

Europe is in the throes of rising anti-Semitism and anti-Islamic sentiment. Perhaps the most visible evidence of this are the legal and political scuffle over whether young Muslim women can wear headscarves in the classroom and the growth of neo-Nazis in Germany. The failure of Europe to find a comfortable place for its substantial Muslim population within its several societies is particularly worrisome. Meanwhile, political Islam as an expression of fundamentalism and nationalism is popping onto the radar screen in Islamic nations as well as ones with large Muslim minorities. In many areas this fundamentalism is anti-modern, anti-Western, and anti-Israel. It may be building towards a growing militancy.

Each statement of intolerance carries with it societal damage. They create canyons, not bridges. Each implicitly encourages a refusal to understand and a willingness to enable violence. Each shreds polities and fosters enclaves. By doing all these things, each retards dialogue or interaction. Western civilization has achieved its greatest dynamism through inclusion. Exclusion, if it becomes a widespread reality, is likely to precipitate its decline.

---

[1] Saint Thomas Aquinas (1225-1274), *Samma Theologiae* II-II q. 11 a. 3, trans. Thomas Gilby (London: Blackfriars, 1964), XXVII, 89, as quoted in Keith Wood *Religion and Community*, (Oxford: Clarendon Press, 2000), p. 108.

[2] Pope Urban II speaking in Clermont, France on November 27, 1095, launched the First Crusade with these words which called for a Truce of God so Christian warriors could reclaim the Holy Land by conquering its Muslim occupiers: "They [Christian barons] should leave off slaying each other and light instead a righteous war, doing the work of God, and God would lead them. For those who died in battle there would be absolution and the remission of sins."

[3] *Gnosticism* was a philosophical or intellectual form of worship which held that knowledge (*gnosis* in Greek) of the true world of God, as opposed to the false, material world created by Satan, was possessed by a small elite who had received this gift through God's messenger, Jesus Christ. *Docetism* held that the realm of matter, or flesh, was different from and opposed to the world of the spirit. Consequently, Jesus was entirely spiritual and never actually inhabited the material world.

[4] For more on this subject see:

> Jason David Be Duhn, *The Manichaean Body*, (Baltimore: Johns Hopkins University Press, 2000).
>
> Pierre Mandonnet, *St. Dominic and His Work*, trans. M. B. Larkin (London, 1945).
>
> Zoe Oldenbourg, *Massacre at Montsegur*, trans. Peter Green (London 1941).

[5] For more on this subject see:

> David Benjamin and Steven Simon, *The Age of Sacred Terror*, (New York: Random House, 2002).
>
> Mark Jueergensmeyer, *Terror in the Mind of God: The Global Rise of Religious Violence*, (Berkeley: University of California Press, 2000).

[6] *Coge intrare* were the words translated as "compel" rather than "invite" as other translations have intimated.

[7] Martin Luther denounced the sale of indulgences by the Catholic Church. He nailed his theses on this and other religious matters to the door of Wittenberg Castle in 1517. This event is considered a reasonable date to point to as the start of the Reformation.

[8] The Protestant Union had been formed in May 1608 by Frederick IV (father of Frederick V) who was Elector of the Palatinate, an area of Germany extending eastward from the Rhine. Maximilian I who was Duke of Bavaria, formed the League of Catholic States, commonly referred to either as the "German Catholic League" or simply the "Catholic League," two months later.

[9] Gustavus II (Adolphus) ruled from (1611 to 1632, he was succeeded by Queen Christina, who ruled from 1632 to her abdication in 1654. This queen was succeeded by: Charles X (1654-1660), Charles XI (1660-1697), and another great warrior Charles XII (1697-1718). Sweden extended its influence over Norway, Finland, Denmark, Poland, and the Baltic States. Charles XII made several incursions into Russia, and his defeat by Peter the Great's forces at the battle of Poltava in 1709 marked the beginning of the decline of Swedish influence in the north.

[10] A study entitled *Too Young to Notice?: The Cultural and Political Awareness of 5-6 Year Olds in Northern Ireland*, was authored by Paul Connolly, Alan Smith, and Bernie Kelly. It was commissioned by the government-funded Community Relations Council, supervised by the University of Ulster, and published on June 25, 2002.

[11] Azar Nafisi, *Reading Lolita in Teheran* (New York: Random House, 2003), p. 273.

[12] Pankaj Mishra, *Murder in India*, review of "'We Have No Orders to Save You': State Participation and Complicity in Communal Violence in Jujarat" a report by Human Rights Watch, *The New York Review of Books*, April 15, 2002, pp. 34-38.

[13] Brian Victoria, *Zen at War*, (Weatherhill Publishers, 1997).

[14] Brian Victoria, *Zen War Stories*, (Taylor and Francis, Inc., 2003).

[15] For a fuller discussion of Sri Lankan religious conflicts see: Martin E. Marty and R. Scott Appleby, editors, *Fundamentalism and the State,: Remaking Polities, Economies and Militance,* (University of Chicago Press, 1993) (Volume 3 of "The Fundamentalism Project"), pp. 589-619.

[16] *Ibid.*

[17] This was the more ascetic form of Buddhism developed by Monks in the fifth to tenth centuries, as opposed to the less strict, more popular Mahayana variety.

[18] For a complete study of this era see Maria Rosa Menocal, *The Ornament of the World*, (Little Brown and Company, 2002).

[19] Arianism was named for the third century North-African prelate, Arius. It was a widespread belief system, which arose within the early Christian church. Arianism denied the full divinity of Christ (who was nevertheless referred to by the Arians as the "Son of God"), who was considered to be a creation of God for a specific salvific purpose.

[20] The Caliph was the religious and leader of the Muslim community acting as the successor to the Prophet Muhammad who was God's Messenger. The Prophet's close companion Abu Babar became the first Caliph after his death in 632 CE. Over the years the succession created disputes and dissention. The most prominent of which was the establishment of Shi'ism in opposition to Sunni conception of the proper lines of control descending from the Prophet. The last Caliphate, the Ottoman, was abolished in 1924.

[21] Tenth Islamic Summit of the Organization of the Islamic Conference, October, 2003 with the full text available at www.adl.org/Antisemitism/Malaysian.ASP.

[22] *Ibid.*

[23] *Ibid.*

[24] See Los Angeles Times, October 16, 2003.

[25] *Ibid.*

[26] *Ibid.*

Chapter Four

Truths

Because thy truth, O Lord, does not belong to me, to this man or that man, but to us all, thou has called us to it with a terrible warning not to claim it exclusively for ourselves, for if we do, we shall lose it.

Saint Augustine
Confessions 12:25

Belief in an absolute truth is the essence of many faiths. For those who are convinced that absolutes flourish, proposals advocating relativism arouse fervent objections. Conversely, those who rely upon reason, or those who see everything as being open to question, regard insistence upon absolutes as being needlessly stubborn.

As a civilization our task is to determine whether there is enough common ground surrounding the subject of truth to entice a majority of those not mired at either end of faith's spectrum. For it is on the verdant pastures of common ground that tolerance has its best opportunity to thrive. This determination will require us to inspect the nature of truth as a concept, and in the process address several questions.[1]

Must an absolute truth be accepted without the possibility of definitional refinement? Most religions would say no, and would encourage some debate, within limits. Does reason have any role in the identification of the absorption of absolute truth? As we will learn, some faiths provide reason with an important role. Can an absolute truth retain its value if it is individual or communal, or does it have to be universal to be valid? This is a hard one, because most faiths consider their truths to be of universal applicability, while realizing that this goal is likely to be unattainable. Finally, our central question is whether members of a particular belief system can accept another system's truth as valid for it even though this truth might contradict what that system deems essential for its members' salvation? The answer as far as it is able to go defines the prospects for tolerance.

Most of us would accept that there is a difference between something that is accepted on faith as an absolute truth, and something for which there is an empirical method for establishing its veracity. However, things are not quite so simple. While reason, or the mind, plays a major role in verification, and emotion, or the heart, plays a major role in acceptance on faith, every belief contains some mixture of the two.

Daoists, for example, praise the mixture. "In this classical Chinese worldview broadly conceived, the mind cannot be divorced from the heart. There are no altogether rational thoughts devoid of feeling, nor any raw feelings altogether lacking in cognitive content."[2] It would be reasonable to conclude, at least under this worldview, that any truth, absolute or not, is a blend containing some degree of feeling and some degree of cognitive content. The precise mixture depends upon both individuals and cultures. Thus, the products may differ while the processes are similar.

Clearly, belief systems will have their own sets of truths and absolute truths. Some of these truths may be considered essential to the attainment of salvation. It would be perfectly natural for belief systems to disagree over the validity and application of particular heart-mind mixtures. It is also to be expected that fervent believers will attempt to persuade others to acknowledge the superiority of their truths. What is not a logical expectation is suppression or repression on account of held beliefs. On many occasions throughout history the perceived threat from another's truth has prompted an intolerant, discriminatory, or even a violent reaction on the part of someone, or some group, striving to protect its own perceived version of truth.

A quotation from Walter M. Miller Jr.'s novel, *A Canticle for Liebowitz*, illustrates this type of religious clash, echoed in the book of *Revelation* and its tales of the Apocalypse, which brings a new truth to prominence.

> Tomorrow a new prince shall rule. Men of understanding, men of science shall stand behind his throne, and the universe will come to know his might. His name is Truth. His empire shall encompass the Earth. And the mastery of Man over the Earth shall be renewed…It will come to pass by violence and upheaval, by flame and by fury, for no change comes calmly over the world.[3]

Truth in this case, and in many cases, may not have been religious but the process of ascension is similar. Its triumph follows in the wake of many prophecies, however, and underscores the struggle's intensity where perceived truth is at stake. Truth, especially one proclaimed absolute, has always been at once blazingly clear and frustratingly elusive. Its volatile mixture of heart and mind has created that effect. Our challenge as a civilization, a nation, and as individuals is to employ enough understanding to defuse truth's more unfortunate characteristics without descending into the morass of anarchy.

DEFINITIONS AND PERSPECTIVES

Truth can be defined, and looked at, in many ways from many vistas. Sir Richard Francis Burton the English explorer, diplomat, author, and mystic summarized a common characteristic that can greatly affect perception of the truth. "Truth is the shattered mirror strown in myriad bits; while each believes his little bit the whole to our own."[4] Such a view not only is common but it also works against tolerance by assisting the growth of militant insularity.

For millennia philosophers and theologians of many faiths have struggled to find the borders and the depths of truth. Buddhists believe that the Dharma, the collected teachings of *the* Buddha or of *a* Buddha, describes the true nature of things, in effect the law of the cosmos.[5] Hsing Yan notes the difficulty of getting a grip on it.

> The Dharma is the truth. Because it is true, the Dharma cannot be contained in a single summation. Nor can it ever be captured in some formula abstracted from philosophical language. As soon as we are sure that we have grasped it, the Dharma slips away again. This is so because the moment we teach one of its truths, we ourselves begin to change. The moment light shines in darkness is gone. The shadowy hand that held the light is gone.[6]

For followers of this concept, absolute truth, or a truth, can exist, but can never be precisely defined. A similarly fluid situation persists on the border between science and mysticism. "You are anti-Mystical, I propose, to the extent that you think reality has been or can be explained, and I mean really explained, by Hinduism or theosophy or gnosticism or superstring theory or any other theory or theology."[7] On the spiritual side of the border, truth or reality, to the extent that it exists, is intensely personal, a shard of Burton's shattered mirror.

As noted above, over the years philosophers have articulated the ways they perceive truth. A glance at five of these attempts provides additional infrastructure for piecing together an overview.[8]

Pythagoras: "Mathematics is, I believe, the chief source of the belief in eternal and exact truth."

Heraclitus: "No man is likely to have arrived at complete and final truth on any subject whatever."

Protagoras: "the pursuit of truth, when it is whole-hearted, must ignore moral considerations; we cannot know in advance what the truth will turn will turn out to be."

Hegel: He envisioned a continual evolution of truth through a dialectical process in which opposite states of being constantly contend, dismantling old ideas and producing new ones. "Truth is the unity of the universal and subjective will."

Simone Weill: "No widely held belief is totally lacking in truth."

The view that truth is a laser beam of clarity and immutability has also been prevalent throughout the ages. In September, 2000 Cardinal Joseph Ratzinger, then head of the Catholic Church's Congregation for the Doctrine of the Faith, and now Pope Benedict XVI, published a thirty-six page thesis entitled *Dominus Jesus: On the Unicity and Salvific Universality of Jesus Christ and the Church*. This work asserts as a doctrinal fact that the exclusive ecclesiastical home for the deposit of the fullness of Christian truth lies within the Catholic Church.

Elaine Pagels traces the founding of this doctrine defining unique and universal truth to the second century.[9] Bishop Irenaeus of Lyons, and others, consolidated the faith building a clerical hierarchy in the process. The solidifying element was adherence to the exclusive ecclesiastical home and its Christian truth. The policy begun at that time was hardened under Emperor Constantine with the help of key church officials, among them Athanasius, intermittently Bishop of Alexandria. It can be argued that a strict definition of truth was key to the survival of Christianity. It provided the mortar that produced a degree of unity from existing fragments.

Thomas Merton, a mystical Trappist monk, a seeker of an absolute, unifying truth, had a slightly different perspective.

> The Truth man needs is not a philosopher's abstraction, but God himself. The paradox of contemplation is that God is never really known unless He is also loved. And we cannot love Him unless we do His will. This explains why modern man, who knows so much is nevertheless ignorant. Because he is without love, modern man fails to see the only Truth that matters and on which all else depends.[10]

Tibetan Buddhists also venerate an absolute truth with universal application. "Absolute truth is the freedom from all elaborations and judgments, and is the object of self-awareness discriminatory wisdom. The wisdom is the undeluded insight that transcends expression and conceptions."[11] There is no question that there are many clear visions of absolute truth. The questions about tolerance arise when, like pebbles cast into a still pond, their ripples interact.

Scientists can look for indivisible truths as well, but their methods can lean heavily on the rational. Edward O. Wilson advocates bypassing philosophy and faith in the search.

> No one should suppose that objective truth is impossible to attain, even when the most committed philosophers urge use to acknowledge that incapacity. In particular, it is too early for scientists, the foot soldiers of epistemology, to yield ground so vital to their mission. Although seemingly chimerical at times, no intellectual vision is more important and daunting that that of objective truth based on scientific understanding.[12]

Roger Bacon's *Opus Maius* of 1258 expressed concern that truth would be continually become obsoleted by new discovery. "Argument brings conclusions and compels us to concede them, but it does not cause certainty nor remove doubts in order that the mind may remain at rest in truth, unless this is provided by experience."[13] He advocated putting every religious contention through scientific tests to establish its validity.

Bacon's continual obsolescence of truth is almost post-modern in its conception. Michael Foucault, as paraphrased by Paul Robinson is deconstructionalist, but not all that far from Bacon. "Foucault is highly suspicious of claims to universal truths...For Foucault there is no external position of certainty, no universal understanding that is beyond history and society."[14]

It is possible to be ecumenical without being relativist. Elizabeth Sifton, quoting her father theologian Reinhold Niebuhr, articulates this view. "Truth is many sided, even Christian truth. We ought to be tolerant with people who see the truth a little bit differently than we do and who worship with slightly different forms."[15]

I am encouraged by those who have had the courage to pursue tolerance in the realm of truth even under extreme pressure. Iranian reformer Abdul Karim Soroush spoke out in the crucible of fundamental Shi'ism. "No one is perfect enough to have an absolute claim on understanding the truth...and no single understanding of Islam is automatically more correct or definitive than another."[16]

We have glanced at a few perspectives on the subject of truth. The many quotes reflect considerable differences. Some of these expressions went farther than do most religious truth-seekers who tend to remain within the bounds of their faiths. Whatever the result, the quest is the same: define faith or discover truth. Human beings have been engaged in this task forever, with widely varying results. All faiths have participated in the attempt to define truth. Nonetheless, no definition has emerged that all have accepted. On many occasions truths proclaimed by others have been fiercely resisted. These occasions tend to capture the headlines of history. It is not usually considered "news" when the religious view of others have been tolerated, if not accepted. But these are the periods worthy of study and emulation.

THE MISTS OF TRUTH

All of us have grown accustomed to hear the latest versions of "absolute" truth proclaimed from pulpits and platforms, supported by pages of text. However, history reveals a kaleidoscope of passages from the *Bible* or the *Koran*, some of which are contradictory, precipitating the changing rhythms of belief. The messages themselves often vary from translation to translation, and edition to edition.

Indisputably, the original Muslims or Christians would barely recognize some of the tenets currently uttered in their founder's name. Fyodor Dostoevsky made this point dramatically in Book Five, Chapter Five of The Brothers Karamazov (published in 1880). One of the brothers (Ivan) tells another (Aloysha) a tale of a sixteenth century Spanish Grand Inquisitor who arrests, reprimands and banishes a retuned Jesus for upsetting a subdued populace by putting dangerous (to the church hierarchy) ideas into their heads. He implies that the Christianity of Seville in the 1550s or Saint Petersburg in the   1880s is materially different from what existed in first century Palestine. Time and time again what are presented as bedrock principles are the product of an almost imperceptible progressions, subtly employed to meet present conditions through adaptable interpretations.

Fundamentalists of different stripes try to give the impression of a return to immutable basic truths that have been unfortunately eroded by modernity. But the values that they believe to be essential for salvation are themselves the result of numerous alterations and addenda that can camouflage interpretive movement.[17] Thus, an often-unrecognized characteristic of perceived truth is that beneath its stony façade lies a fluid layer of principles.

The methods used to locate and to promulgate truth are almost as varied as the perceptions themselves. Technology has provided considerable flexibility to those wishing to get their message out. While a message may be based upon a text that must be accepted as presented, there are considerable differences in the spirit with which the message is offered. The attitude displayed by those considering a particular belief, or set of beliefs, essential to their salvation is altered if they actively proselytize and altered further if discrimination or persecution is involved.

The process of locating perceived truth has remained more consistant. Some find it in texts. Some meditate. Some employ visions. There are other ways as well, but the search depends upon depth of belief (even if it is scientific). The challenges of every culture, and most particularly for ours, are to convert the emotion of deeply held beliefs into a uniting rather than a dividing force. Should that complex task be accomplished the mists of truth could part revealing understanding and tolerance.

THE PROCESS OF UNITING

Aside from the pure intellectual effort expended in learning about various systems and their perceptions of truth there are some emotional avenues that can lead in the general direction of tolerance.

MYSTICISM

Mysticism for our purposes can be defined as: "The practice of putting oneself into and remaining in direct relation with God the Absolute, or any unifying principle of life."[18] Mystics in every faith possess these general characteristics. For some mystics, God exists outside of the individual and often outside of the universe. For them in order to have unity the human essence (sometimes called the soul) has to rise, perhaps in stages, to meld with the divine. For others, God is present deep within one's essence and discovery requires intense introspection. Still others seek to bring divinity to them from above or beyond. Mystics seek unifying principles. Thus, they usually tend to be more accepting of those on similar quests, albeit, within different belief systems.

The mystic process works toward establishment of a unifying wholeness and oneness. "It is our standing-out (ex-sistentia) from the primordial wholeness of all things in God which breaks our union with him."[19] Obviously, it is not always the case, but someone trying to find unity may be more willing to countenance those who believe differently and not attempt to impose unity with the divine though a particular set of beliefs, History has borne out this general assumption. Let us take a brief look at three biographical examples of mystical approaches.

Yahya Suhrawardi was born in Persia in 1155 CE. He developed a theosophy of Light that welded mysticism to philosophy. The philosophy in his case was Zoroastrian Neoplatonism. The mysticism was the metaphysical ecstasy associated with light.[20] Suhrawardi based his beliefs on the Platonic devotion to ethical and religious ideals, united by The One, who was only accessible through abstract thought. He employed the concept of Zoroastrian angelology as a metaphysical connector. Suhrawardi called the One, or Perfect Man, the Sage. He provided universal linkage between philosophical principles and mystical ecstasy, which merged in the creative imagination. Despite the peaceful nature of what later became Shi'ite Sufism, Suhrawardi was executed by order of the Sunni Muslim clerics in the government of Saladin in 1191 CE.

The French Jesuit Pierre Teilhard de Chardin (1891-1955) was a scientist of note, in geology, paleontology, and archeology. He also became a revered philosopher when his work was posthumously published.[21] His mysticism envisioned all of humanity and their religions, unified by an anthropomorphic Christ figure acting as a magnetic symbol. Teilhard believed that subliminal energy would erase the contradictions between the physical and psychic worlds. They would grow progressively closer together through a process he called noogenesis.[22] Teilhard wrote of a world filled with love and tolerance, which was remarkable since much of his work was done during the destructive chaos of World War II. He expected the ultimate truth to be the mystical energy contained in the anthropomorphic symbol of Christ, which would be God's ultimate revelation. This truth would be the direct link between each one of them and God.

Two Spanish mystics who were associates, Saint Teresa of Avila (1515-1582) and Saint John of the Cross (1500-1569) were involved in the reform of the monastic movement in that country. They were Carmelites interested in establishing a stricter, simpler form of monastic observance that was described as *discalced*.[23] Not unlike the Spiritual Franciscans they advocated poverty and less reliance on church bureaucracy by communicating directly with God. Both were tireless workers and were skilled, prolific writers. Saint Teresa claimed to feel the presence of Christ inside herself, which she radiated in her speech and writings. The traditional Carmelite hierarchy, who quite naturally felt threatened, intermittently chastened both.

Personal contact with God that does not require interlocutors is one of the features of mysticism that can make it more tolerant. So can its frequent use of symbolism. These features are not an unmixed blessing. Mentors or gurus usually guide mystics so there is room for abuse or intolerance. Symbolism can foster a requirement for elite knowledge, to decipher what were often protective mechanisms. Thus, there is no guarantee that mystics will be more pacific and tolerant than their mainstream cousins. But in general, mysticism can be a tempering factor, permitting more understanding through their ideas of unity from the inside outward.

ANTHROPOMORPHISM AND MYTHICAL FIGURES

Anthropomorphism is a common method for divine portrayal and for the creation of unity among believers. As animism developed into organized religions (albeit with an animistic cast) the concept of anthropomorphism began to surface as a way to depict divinity. Although animistic practices, such as Druids worshipping spirits in trees, and partially animistic figures, such as the elephant-headed Ganesh the Hindu god of wisdom, or Sakaret the part lioness Egyptian god of war, human-like objects of worship became gradually more prevalent.

Naturally, human beings can more easily conceptualize and identify with deities who are somewhat similar to them. Often it helps people grasp divinity if the figure is believed to have supernatural or superhuman powers. Almost every faith encompasses some sort of semi-human, possibly mythological, figures with miraculous abilities. The Greek, Roman, Vedic or Viking pantheon of gods fits this description as does the enlightened Buddha, the Prophet Mohammed, Jesus Christ, and the several forms of angelology, all of which require divinity to assume human form at some stage.

Art, architecture, and literature frequently present divinities anthropomorphically and mythologically, as if to present focal points for unified worship. The line between truth and symbolism within a believer's imagination is sometimes indistinct. So is the border between history and myth, which makes these divinities so much larger than life, and so appealing.

A considerable body of work has been devoted to the discovery of the historical Jesus, or Mohammed, or Buddha, or some other important religious figure. These works more often than not fail to connect the sketchy historical facts with the objects of worship. Truth is indeed elusive, but it is hard to escape the reality of the images within the believers' minds, whether they can be historically verified or not.

Even when facts are available, attempts can be made to conceal or de-emphasize them if they are deemed to be adverse. How meaningful are the personal lives of various Popes? Saint Augustine held that the worth or interests of the church as a whole outweighed the actions of any of its representatives. Yet, major reactions or schisms resulted from the intemperate leaders. The Council of Torah Sages of Agudath Israel of America banned a book on the personal lives of esteemed Torah scholars.[24] Would exposing their lives dilute their message? The Council thought so.

Mythology and anthropomorphism can lead down strange paths when their underlying precepts become intertwined with humanity. Can the essence be divorced from the messenger? Can the nature of the messenger distort the purity of the conveyed truth? Can the separation of myth from history make the message more powerful?

Mysticism attempts to unite God with individuals. Fundamentalism attempts to connect basic values with incidents in individual lives. Anthropomorphism and mythology attempt to put divinity into forms or terms individuals can recognize. All are attempts to unite. Unfortunately, the transposition required often divides, as it struggles to offer basics simple enough to be understood by vast numbers of people. Perhaps broad unity is fleeting, if so, we will have to look in other places for tolerance.

SCIENCE VERSUS FAITH[25]

The ageless conflict between science and faith for claming rights to truth has been resumed. In recent years the conflict has increased with the battleground being evolution as presented by Charles Darwin, among others. From the moment it emerged from Darwin's brain his theory has been controversial, especially among people of faith.

At present there are two extreme camps, with a large and complex middle. One extreme sees any attack upon Darwin as the explanation for how our species, or any species, evolved as the beginning of the end of science. The other extreme regards any explanation of evolution that does not include God as being the beginning of the end of faith, and therefore invalid. The middle, a little surprised and more than a little perplexed scrambles to find some grounds for compromise that can survive political as well as academic tests. Accusations of atheism and irrational belief fly back and forth, causing all participants to duck frequently. Many academics are convinced that mere feelings, which are at the heart of religion, cannot possibly discover genuine truth. Many sincere believers cannot accept any version of truth based solely upon scientific principles.

On one side of the present conflict are creationists and their cohorts, or successors, those who propose a theory called Intelligent Design. Theologically speaking, creationism as a religious topic was initially advanced by such figures as Saints Jerome and Thomas Aquinas. This theory held that a new soul was created for each individual. It differed from the Traducianism of Tertullian, which postulated that souls were inherited from parents. This version of Creationism was widely accepted by the Catholic Church.

The more recent meaning of creationism stems from the concept of *creation ex nihilo* which asserts that not only did God create the universe and everything in it, but also that it was created from nothing. Some creationists have also insisted upon biblical not anthropological dating and benchmarks. Neo-creationists modify this somewhat to allow for more ancient origins of the planets and the universe. A more recent modification, Intelligent Design, proponents go one step further, and while accepting scientific dating and some aspects of evolution, claim that living organisms are so complex that they cannot be completely explained by science. God must have been the designer. They advocate that Intelligent Design be taught as a potential alternative to evolution.

The issue in the United States is not merely one of belief it has political ramifications as well. Creationism garnered some political support for its attempt to be included in educational curricula, but it seemed too radical to many. On the other hand, Intelligent Design's proponents are attempting to achieve its inclusion by asserting that evolution doesn't have all the answers and plausible alternatives need to be explored as well. Whether this approach is being used as a "wedge" to eventually separate evolution from the educational mainstream and provide room for the eventual acceptance of the entire Creationist agenda depends on who is asked. What is evident is the attempt to break evolution's monopoly hold on explanations of species development.

Terry Fox, pastor of the largest Southern Baptist congregation in the Midwest, in Wichita, Kansas, supports the "wedge". "The strategy this time is not to go for the whole enchilada. We're trying to be a little more subtle. If you believe God created that baby, it makes it a whole lot harder to get rid of that baby. If you can cause enough doubt on evolution, liberalism will die."[26] On the other hand, there are those like John F. Haught, Director of the Georgetown University Center for the Study of Science and Religion, who was cited above, that believe the addition of God would provide needed depth to explanations of the universe and human development. In any event, four states and a number of municipalities have either included, or are seriously considering, inclusion of Intelligent Design in their textbooks as a part of the curriculum.

The Discovery Institute in Seattle carries out a well-financed effort to instill the view that evolution is just one theory among many. The National Center for Science Education is equally enthusiastic in its warnings that Intelligent Design is just a smoke screen for creationism. Atheists and agnostics bristle at any hint that God might have a role to play in what should remain a purely scientific process. The battle continues to rage.[27]

Philip Kitcher outlines how certain procedures could be applied to both sides so that the most fertile discussions can take place in the middle ground.

> A first sobering thought is that realism is dogmatism by a nicer name. Claiming that the sciences tell us the truth in particular cases can easily sound like a refusal to countenance alternatives...To claim the truth of a statement is not to declare the certainty of our knowledge...Indeed, we spend our lives proclaiming true. and acting upon beliefs we recognize as vulnerable in the course of future experience. There is no snapping shut of our minds, no insulation against critical scrutiny. when we move from saying we believe to declaring its truth...Part of the critical attitude should lead us to inquire if the rival views, based on different experiences, provide grounds for revising or enriching our beliefs.[28]

In the next chapter we will explore a mechanism that offers a role for God in science. Meanwhile, we need to keep searching for ways to marginalize the two extremes, to keep the channels of communication open, and to prevent the science versus faith debate from overflowing into the realm of politics or the process of government.

POSTMODERN TRUTH

The academic discipline of postmodernism, with its often-employed technique of deconstruction, has set itself up as an alternative to absolute immutable truth. Three descriptions provide a sketch of what its concepts are about.

"Postmodernism is the conception that all understanding is conditioned historically and culturally, and that moral principles are grounded in communities rather than in the nature of things. Postmodernism challenges the sense of being in agreement with an objective world."[29]

"Deconstruction…this is the attempt to take apart a particular position, its assertions and arguments, in order to discover within it conflicting elements. The assumption here is that a text has conflicting elements of significance within it, because it signifies in more than one way."[30]

> Truth must be seen in a different fashion. In particular, postmodernism rejects epistemological realism, a correspondence view of truth, a referential understanding of language and foundationalism in epistemology. In the place of correspondence to reality, postmodernism often substitutes one of two options. One alternative is a coherence view of truth, the idea that the test of truth is to be found by taking our ideas as a whole, not atomistically, and checking the coherence of the set of propositions. The other option is the use of a pragmatic view of truth, namely the idea that truth is that which works, or enables us to make progress toward mutually agreed on goals.[31]

In some important characteristics postmodernism has similarities to Daoism which is a search for the way (dao) and which provides a basic sense of equilibrium (jing). This is achieved via a processual worldview, which strings a series of events together.

"These processual events are porous, flowing into each other in the ongoing transformations we call experience."[32]

"The field of experience is always construed from one perspective or another. There is no view from nowhere, no external perspective, no decontextualized vantage point."[33]

As we will see in the next chapter when we discuss quantum theory, there are opinions that "reality" or "truth" are constantly changing phenomena. They apply to particular individuals in particular contexts but are not necessarily broadly applicable, or valid for extensive periods of time. What might be valid for one person at one time might not be valid for another person at the same time or the same person at a later time.

Thus, a postmodern, a Dao, or a quantum truth has properties differing from those held by many belief systems. It is clear that there is no single worldwide position on truth, or even general agreement that truth exists.

The world's task is how to accommodate these various positions, which are inherently in disagreement, without resorting to discrimination, repression or violence. It is not an easy task and it will require the normally passive moderate majority to become proactive in order to marginalize the extremes.

---

[1] For a more detailed discussion of this and related subjects see: *Simon Blackburn, Truth: A Guide to the Perplexed,* (London: Oxford University Press, 2005).

[2] Roger T. Ames and David L. Hall, translation and commentary, *Dao De Jing: Making Life Significant*. (New York: Ballantine Books, 2003) p. 26.

[3] Walter M. Miller, Jr., *A Canticle for Leibowitz*, (Philadelphia: J. B. Lippencott Company, 1960) p. 206.

[4] The Kasidah of Haji Abdn, El Yazdi I, 33.

[5] For Hindus Dharma defines the right way of living and as such became one of the pillars supporting the caste system.

[6] Hsing Yan, *Lotus in a Stream*, trans. by Tom Graham, (New York: Weatherhill, 2000) p. 19.

[7] John Horgan, *Rational Mysticism: Dispatched from the Border, between Science and Spirituality*, (Boston: Houghton Mifflin, 2003) p. 217.

[8] Pythagoras (570-500 BCE): Born in Samos, he founded a philosophical school in Crotona, Italy. This school believed in gender equity, communal property, vegetarianism, transmigration, and salvation through the quest for truth.

Heraclitas (540-475 BCE): Born in Ephesus, he believed all things are in a state of flux and conflict out of which develops true value.

Protagoras (490-410 BCE): Born in Thrace, he was the most significant of the Sophists who held that individual perceptions were all valid even though they were different.

George William Fredrich Hegel (1770-1831): Born in Stuttgart he did most of his work in Berlin. His new-rationalist idealism envisioned a polarized universe. The history of its evolution provided a guide for determining the present.

Simone Weill (1909-1943): Born in Paris into the Jewish faith, she was influenced by her studies of Christian and Hindu mysticism.

[9] See Elaine Pagels, *Beyond Belief*, (New York: Random House, 2003) pp. 80-113.

[10] Thomas Merton, *The Ascent to Truth*, (New York: Harcourt Brace and Company, 1951) p. 10.

[11] Tulku Thondup Rinpoche, *Hidden Teachings of Tibet*, edited by Harold Talbott, (Boston: Wisdom Publications, 1986) p. 23.

[12] Edward O. Wilson, *Consilience: The Unity of Knowledge*, (Alfred A. Knopf, 1998) p. 61.

[13] Roger Bacon, *Opus Maius*

[14] Paul Robinson, editor, *The Foucault Reader*, (New York: Pantheon Books, 1984) p. 4.

[15] Elizabeth Sefton, *The Serenity Prayer*, (New York: W. W. Norton & Company, 2003) p. 99.

[16] Robin Wright, *The Last Great Revolution: Turmoil and Transformation in Iran*, (Alfred A. Knopf, 2000) p. 52.

[17] Liberal Catholic theologian Hans Küng addressed this issue in his book, *My Struggle for Freedom*, (Wm. B. Eerdmans, Grand Rapids, MI, 2002). He employed the word catholic as taken from the Greek katholicos to mean "that which forms a whole". This quote comes from p. 225, "We need not immediately give up on the unity of scripture and New Testament canon of scripture simply because of all the differences...Rather, it dawns on me that a reshaping, development and revision of the original message, depending on the changing situations in which rte author preached and of their communities, was absolutely necessary, this in particular gives us today the opportunity once again to translate the original Christian message into a new situation of preaching instead of merely repeating it word forward, to interpret it in a way which accords with the time."

[18] Fifth edition of the *Columbia Encyclopedia*.

[19] Simon Tugwell in the preface to *The Cloud of the Unknown*, James Walsh, ed. (Mahwah, NJ: Paulist Press, 1981) p. xxi.

[20] For more on Suhrawardi and his mysticism see: Henry Corbin, *The Man of Light in Iranian Sufism* (New York: Omega Publications, 1978). *The History of Islamic Philosophy*, edited by Seyyed Hossein Nasr and Oliver Leaman (London: Rutledge, 1996) is also helpful on this subject.

[21] One collection of his essays, trans. by René Hague, is called *Activation of Energy* (New York: Harcourt Brace Jovanovich, 1971).

[22] Noology is the science of understanding. Genesis means a coming into being, or origin.

[23] The term discalced literally means shoeless and represents a stricter, simpler form of monastic rule.

[24] Rabbi Nathan Kanenetky, *Making of a Godol: A Study in the Lives of the Great Torah Personalities*, (New York: 2003).

[25] For a more complete discussion of this topic four books stand out:

Ian G. Barbour, *When Science Meets Religion*, (New York: Harper Collins, 2000)

John F. Haught, *Deeper than Darwin*, (Boulder CO: Westview Press, 2003)

Kenneth R. Miller, *Finding Darwin's God*, (New York: Harper Collins, 1999)

Gerald L. Schroeder, *The Hidden Face of God*, (New York: Simon & Schuster, 2001)

[26] From an article by Peter Sleven in the Washington Post National Weekly Edition of March 21, 2005, p. 6. "The whole enchilada" is Creationism.

[27] Florida State University professor Michael Ruse has written a book on this battle. It is the *Evolution – Creation Struggle*, (Cambridge: Harvard University Press, 2005).

[28] Philip Kitcher, *Science, Truth and Democracy*, (New York: New York University Press, 2001) p. 13.

[29] Millard J. Erickson, *Truth of Consequences: The Promise and Perils of Postmodernism* (Danvers Grove: Illinois University Press, 2001) p. 231.

[30] Ibid, p. 131.

[31] Ibid, p. 232.

[32] *Dao de Jing*, trans. and with commentary by Roger T. Ames and David L. Hall, (New York: Ballantine Books, 2003) p. 19.

[33] Ibid, p. 18.

Chapter Five

Dimensions

William J. Cromie

During the twentieth century some remarkable breakthroughs were made in
the field of physics that changed the way we regard the earth and its surrounding
universe. Some have felt that these breakthroughs widened the existing divisions
between science and faith, in the process lessening the role of God. Physics, like
biology, offers explanations for natural phenomena, many of which previously
dwelt in the realm of religion. However, in addition to opening new vistas for
science, twentieth century physics also provided ample room for God. We
should keep this in mind as we explore some of the territory physics has made
available to us.

PERCEPTIONS OF REALITY

Over the last century a skein of scientific discoveries changed the nature of
biology, chemistry, geology, physics and mathematics. In the process of their
development, they revolutionized the established concepts of reality. As these
concepts changed, perforce many elements of philosophy and belief had to be
reassessed. Some certainties became uncertain. Some absolutes became maybes.
Some perceived truths became opaque. But at the same time other areas,
previously wrapped in a fog of doubts and questions, were clarified.

As an illustration it might be helpful to look at the way people perceive. It has become evident that what we have always envisioned as the seamless passage of time could well be an illusion created by a series of discrete snapshots that give the mind an impression of continuity. Furthermore, magnetic resonance imagery (MRI) monitoring of brain cell activity appears to reveal that each individual develops his or her particular method of determining what and how to perceive. Individualized perception incorporates an accumulation of tendencies and experiences that progressively shape what each of us might look at and understand from the things we "see".

Starting in the late nineteenth century, scientists began to suspect that human beings "saw" images in a way that resembled cinematography. This suspicion was reinforced as observations of people who suffered from migraines, strokes, and seizures revealed that they occasionally endured extended periods when their perceptual snapshots did not advance. In effect, they went into a freeze frame mode where "time" stood still.

Some of the best work on this subject has been done by Christof Koch and Francis Crick (co-discoverer of DNA).[2] They postulated that what we considered conscious awareness actually consists of a series of static snapshots with motion "painted" on them. This conclusion can be interpreted to mean that in each individual brain, billions of nerve cells are firing volleys at each other causing development of a personal version of continuity, rather than a generalized packet of snapshots available to be viewed by all.

In other words, two people could be sitting side by side near a house gazing out over the water, but would "see" slightly different "paintings" of flowing waves and passing boats. Either of their minds would absorb minutely dissimilar still pictures that form panoramas the exact contents of which largely depend upon their personal history of perceptions and proclivities. Unhappily, one of them might suffer a physical trauma while sitting which could provoke a temporary halt in the procession of snapshots, making their side-by-side sensations of "time" materially different.

These ideas about elapsed time are not revolutionary. Albert Einstein completed his special theory of relativity around 1905 and his general theory a decade later. His theories postulated that people would experience time differently based upon their rate of movement relative to each other and introduced the concept of spacetime which became understood as a fourth dimension.

Around the same time, some artists, most notably Pablo Picasso in his work *Les Demoiselles d'Avignon*, began to employ spacetime as a visual enhancement. These artists attempted to portray images as they might be "seen" from the fourth dimension. Needless to say, these images caused both a sensation and violent reactions while turning established conceptions inside out.[3]

Science has gone even further to challenge our accepted notions of time, continuity, and dimensionality. As we have already noted, and will explore later, Werner Heisenberg developed the *uncertainty principle* in 1927, building on work he had done with Neils Bohr. This principle eventually allowed for a possible connection between science and religion. More recently, some scientists have begun to invalidate the concept of time, as we know it.[4] They envision a quantum cosmology in which multiple universes experience only instants in the present, called *nows*, with no pasts or futures.

Further searches through physics for universal explanations have uncovered many, perhaps infinite, dimensions. These dimensions are imbedded in what are called strings or superstrings, which comprise the universe, or universes, as the case may be.[5] As noted above, such new discoveries and ideas have altered the way humans can perceive reality. Changing perceptions can have a profound impact on convictions, and that is our subject.

CERTAINTIES

Belief in God as a manifestation of absolute truth is for many of us the only certainty to which we have clung. It can represent the keystone for constructing personal equilibrium, and any concept, idea, or scientific proof that might shake this belief could be personally cataclysmic. How we as a country, and as a civilization, have reacted and will react to bone rattling developments of this nature goes a considerable way toward defining us.

It is not unusual that scientific frontiers breached in the past few decades have thrown a mantle of doubt over much of what we had assumed about our world and its universe. Conventional thought has been challenged before. As was the case after Galileo's writings, for example, no longer can we be certain about "reality". It has been replaced in many minds by an interlocking series of questions and probabilities.[6] Over the last century these challenges to existing certainties have placed science and faith into opposition. By so doing, they have raised emotional temperatures, often to dangerous levels. What needs to be done is to find mechanisms for lowering temperatures and bridging gaps. This may not turn out to be an impossible task.

Discoveries that open up new areas of inquiry could inspire a review of past contentions and a more generous acceptance of what others might believe. Dismantling or enervating long held beliefs also could cause an opposite reaction. Obviously perceived religious truths have to be approached gingerly, especially where science is involved. Thus any concept that may leave more room for divinity within the envelope of scientific thinking would be welcome.

Belief systems often require a leap of faith to arrive at their versions of truth. These leaps can defy logic. Quantum theory also confronts accepted logic actually assists those attempting to leap. It requires a leap emotionally or mentally to be accepted as a possibility. Brian Green describes the methodology whereby religious certainties can be reinforced by questioning presumed scientific absolutes this is the process, which led to quantum theory.

> The overreaching lesson that has emerged from scientific inquiry over the last century is that human experience is often a misleading guide to the true nature of reality. Lying just beneath the surface of the everyday is a world we'd hardly recognize. Followers of the occult, devotees of astrology, and those who hold to religious principles that speak to a reality beyond experience have, from widely varying perspectives long since arrived at a similar conclusion. But

that's not what I have in mind. I'm referring to the work of ingenious innovators and tireless researchers – the men and women of science – who have peeled back layer after layer of the cosmic onion, enigma by enigma, and revealed a universe that is at once surprising, unfamiliar, exciting, elegant, and thoroughly unlike what anyone ever expected.[7]

Operating in the quantum realm, religious certainties are simultaneously upon both shakier and more solid ground. For individuals, especially those with a mystical bent, the fact that science seems to support personalized perception, alternate "realities", or mysticism could bring science and faith closed together. But for established cadres of structured belief systems the crumbling of some presumed certainties could induce disquieting uncertainty. This was the case with Galileo, with Darwin, and with Einstein.

On balance, challenging presumed certainties should be a positive event. Opening possibilities where closed doors once stood should assist tolerance. All the while acknowledgement that science condones uncertainty, maybe even divinity, could smooth some of the abrasive edges that disrupt rational dialogue between scientists and believers.

> Science and religion both take for granted that the universe is much deeper than it seems. The whole thrust of science, for example, is to dig beneath what appears on the surface of nature. Scientists make a tacit assumption that the world is always more than what first impressions yield. But religion also assumes that there is more to the world than what appears on the surface, indeed infinitely more.[8]

THEORIES REVIEWED

At this point we will get acquainted briefly with several scientific concepts. At times they may seem like science fiction, which is not surprising considering that this genre is often based upon cutting edge research. As mentioned earlier, some of these theories challenge accepted ideas of reality, which in turn could affect the underpinnings of belief or concepts of truth.[9]

Starting in the nineteenth century, and accelerating through most of the twentieth, science began to alter the way many people regarded their beliefs. Science began to add depth to many concepts connected to belief, such as time and the cosmos. Einstein's theories of relativity were a turning point, creating fresh vistas and new directions for perceiving the mechanisms of the universe. General relativity assembled the strands of the previous century's work. Put simply, it postulated that gravitational fields act upon spacetime to warp it. Combined with Einstein's special relativity it allows for different measurements to be applied to separate entities and locations so that neither space nor time (or spacetime) are constant. For example, those hovering in a spaceship at the lip of a black hole (if this were technically feasible) would experience a massive slow down in time relative to those residing on earth. At its core Einstein's revolution with general relativity was to prove that both space and time were flexible, not fixed. That discovery led to some other theories with equally important implications.

Quantum theory was pieced together over the course of the twentieth century to explain the emission and absorption of energy by matter and the motion of material particles. It held that energy is emitted and absorbed in a number of ways. Measurements determined that these minute energy infused particles could only be defined with certainty when they were actually being observed. Quantum mechanics and quantum physics together produced theories revolving around subatomic entities, which depicted a cosmology that defied many previous notions of "reality". If something is provably present only when it is being observed, what is there when it is not being observed? Could it be observed far away only milliseconds later? Could it be in two places at once?

Ironically, these theories provided some credence for many religious practices that had become discredited by the rise of Judeo-Christian orthodoxy as a backbone of Western civilization. For example, time travel and dream travel, along with mystical visions still occupy prominent positions in faiths, but usually not to the degree that prevailed at one time. Acceptance of these phenomena as scientifically possible expressions can transform both the intellectual and the emotional landscape, especially if they begin to seep back into mainstream belief systems.

Similarly, when scientists argue that time, as we conventionally denominate it does not really exist except as some calibration of change, the possibility that their assertion might be correct forces us to consider whether we need to realign our system of measurement. Those of us (like myself) who were born before World War II are likely to have grown up with ideas about hours, miles and history that had been in place for centuries. Relativity was introduced gradually, bending our thoughts about time. Space became delineated, but questions were raised about its origins, its shape, and its future. These questions had both scientific and religious implications. As quantum theory and religious strains were blended slowly into this mix a new concoction emerged in which imagination and perception were often indistinguishable. Certainty became even more of a moving target, even as the pressure to find it intensified.

Question marks were sprayed upon belief replacing many periods. Quite naturally, this inversion disturbed the tranquility of those accustomed to particular absolutes, complicating acceptance. But rather than providing fresh ammunition to science at the expense of faith, quantum theory and its implications may have opened the gate to a bridge between these two often opposed sectors.

> What lies beyond dispute is that the cosmos is endowed with a narrative structure that allows genuinely new things, such as life and evolution, to happen in the course of time. This is not a trait that we can simply take for granted. What will always remain open for theological speculation, therefore, no matter how extensively the particular sciences fill in the gaps at their various levels of explanation, is the question of why nature is made for narrative.[10]

Quantum theory seems to lead the narrative in a different direction, and that direction could bring science closer to faith. Both require what Toynbee called "a willing suspension of disbelief".

DIMENSIONALITY

Einstein's notion of a fourth dimension startled the world in a profound way that was similar to the idea that the world was round not flat or that our solar system was heliocentric. His possibility posed a fundamental challenge to the scientific elite, the religious establishments, and the educated public. As people began to accept a fourth dimension, it began to become evident that the possibility of further dimensionality had to be considered. For those of us practiced in three-dimensional living and thinking, these possibilities were at once intriguing and intimidating. One of the directions Einstein's thinking inspired, quantum theory, may be the most intriguing of all. The possibility of multidimensionality along with different concepts of space and time blurs the traditionally sharp lines dividing science and faith. Recent research has blurred them even more.

String and superstring theory, for instance, require numerous dimensions, most of them sub-microscopic. Parallel universes are becoming a topic in the more esoteric marches of physics. Each of these developments creates more uncertainty about the nature of the cosmos, and thus provides more room for the presence of God.

As conceptual developments, these ideas are not brand new. Previously we discussed Arthur I. Miller's work on perception at the turn of the twentieth century. Nine years before Einstein completed his work on relativity Picasso and his colleagues were wrestling with the visual presentation of multidimensionality to an audience that only accepted three dimensions. Over the years artists, writers and cinematographers as wells as scientists, have wrestled with the meaning of multiple dimensions. So far these efforts have entranced, entertained or repulsed without being integrated into the religious mainstream. This may be about to change through conceptual overlap.

Elements of multidimensionality were always detectible in mystic belief expressions. Hinduism and Buddhism contain multidimensional features. So-called "New Age" beliefs often employ a mechanism called channeling, which is communication with the deceased. Channels speak frequently of the multidimensional aspects of identity, for instance, or the possibility that we are simultaneously co-existing on different planes. This will not be news to many Native Americans, Maya, or a host of other believers who weave ancestor worship, time travel, dream travel, and visions into their faiths. Their worlds are not necessarily three dimensional and the dividing lines between past, present, and future are often indistinct.

Quantum theory further supports the possibility that a particle could be in two places at the same time. It also supports depiction of a multi-dimensional cosmology, even one with multiple universes. These universes could have different characteristics. They could result from a process of continual inflation that constantly creates new entities. They could result from combinations of strings or superstrings consisting of vibrating filaments of energy. They could be parallel or emerging from black holes. All of these possibilities and more have been considered. Nothing has been definitely proven. What is important is that new questions are being asked about daring concepts.

To understand the impact of multidimensionality on our world, consider how a creature from the second dimension (were there one) might perceive a third dimension. Visually, in a second dimension a person or a chair would appear completely flat. Depth and shape would have to be imagined. The third dimension might be proven mathematically, but its appearance would have to be taken on faith, laced with conjecture not conviction. However, once the principle of an additional dimension is accepted it becomes difficult to put a lid on the eventual number of possible dimensions, and hence perceptions.

The same might be said of universes. Once it is assumed that there could be more than one, it becomes difficult to set a limit. Could they be scattered islands within a universal sea? Could they be parallel, but entirely separate? Gnosticism accepted a cosmos with remarkably similar characteristics. Could the universes be completely different in every respect? The answer to all these questions is "yes". Thus, these questions illustrate how science and its quest to understand and explain the cosmos both challenges and coincides with belief. Perhaps the only way to truly understand a multidimensional, multi-universe cosmos is through a fusion of the two. Perhaps science will become more like religion, obviating the need for delineation.

QUANTUM BELIEF

Quantum theory, which has revolutionized the way we asses our surroundings, was developed over the first third of the twentieth century by a group of physicists including Max Planck, Niels Bohr, Louis de Broglie, Erwin Schrödinger and Werner Heisenberg. Heisenberg authored the uncertainty principle, which may have created the potential for divinity in even the most advanced science. Taken together the principles of quantum theory limited the precision possible in certain measurements, thereby erasing the predictability of future states. In other words, since the advent of quantum theory the nature of our physical world has become less certain, as has the ability of science to explain it. The only "reality" is that which is observed at the moment when it is under observation, and uncertainty pervades everywhere. Could it be that religion will become a good fit with this complex and unfinished cosmos.

As quantum theory matured, its links with some belief systems both past and present become more evident.

> Virtually everything we see and touch and feel is made up of particles that have been involved in interactions with other particles right back through time, to the Big Bang in which the universe as we know it came into being. The atoms in my body are made of particles that once jostled in close proximity in the cosmic fireball with particles that form the body of some living creatures of some distant, undiscovered planet. Indeed, the particles that make up my body

once jostled with the particles that make up your body. We are as much parts of a single system as the two photons flying out of the heart of the Aspect experiment.[11]

END OF QUANTUM BELIEFS

If human beings actually inhabit a quantum cosmos deepened by multidimensionality, laced with parallel universes and filled with recirculating particles, then perhaps science and faith are closer than many expect. Maybe we can consider the revolution in physics that began with Einstein's relativity and continued with the uncertainty principle, quantum theory and the various string theories to be almost religious in nature.

Quantum belief does not ignore, or consciously freeze out, other belief systems. On the contrary, it makes ample room for them. As such, it offers hope for an environment where science and faith can converge and coexist. It offers more, a middle ground where tolerance can prevail and God can be acknowledged.

---

[1] William J. Cromie writing in the November 2000 edition of *Harvard College Gazette* about Charles Marcus, professor of physics at Harvard University's recently established Center for Imaging and Meoscale Structures.

[2] Christof Koch, *The Quest for Consciousness: A Neurological Approach* and Francis Crick, *The Astonishing Hypothesis: The Scientific Search for the Soul.*

[3] Arthur I. Miller, *Einstein, Picasso: Space, Time and the Beauty that Causes Havoc,* (New York: Basic Books, 2001)

[4] Julian Barbour, *The End of Time* (New York: Oxford University Press, 2000)

[5] Brian Greene, *The Elegant Universe* (New York: W.W. Norton & Company, 1999)

[6] Brian Greene, on page 177 of his book *The Fabric of the Cosmos* (New York: Alfred A. Knopf, 2004) sums up his questioning. "But of all the discoveries in physics during the last hundred years, quantum mechanics is far and away the most startling, since it undermines the whole conceptual schema of classical physics.

[7] Brian Greene, *The Fabric of the Cosmos* (New York: Alfred A. Knopf, 2004) p 5.

[8] John F. Haught, *Deeper Than Darwin,* (Boulder CO: Westview Press, 2003) p. 27. Another book that covers this subject slightly differently is Ursula Goodenough's, *The Sacred Depths of Nature,* (New York: Oxford University Press, 1998).

[9] Further reading on the subjects contained in this chapter:
Lee Smolin *Three Roads to Quantum Gravity* (New York: Basic Books, 2001)
Arthur I. Miller, *Space, Time and the Beauty that Causes Havoc* (New York, Basic Books, 2001)
Julian Barbour, *The End of the Time: The Next Revolution in Physics* (New York, Oxford U Press, 2000)
Brian Green, *The Elegant Universe* (New York: W.W. Norton & Co., 1999)
John Gribbin, *In Search of Schrodinger's Cat* (New York: Bantam Books, 1984)
Clifford A. Pickover, *Time: A Traveler's Guide* (New York: Oxford U Press, 1998)
Stephen W. Hawking, *A Brief History of Time* (New York: Bantam Books, 1998)

[10] John F. Haught, *Deeper Than Darwin,* (Boulder CO: Westview Press, 2003) p. 63.

[11] Ibid, p. 229. Alain Aspect and colleagues at the University of Paris conducted an experiment involving light proceeding through polarizing filters that confirmed the basic tenets of quantum theory.

Chapter VI

Utopia and the Loa

The greatest human fear is the power of the unknown, and one of the features of the pack, the group, the horde, was to help vanquish that fear, to embed the person in the reassuring illusion of belonging.

Elias Canetti (1905-1994)

As alluded to earlier, a great many people throughout the world believe that spirits of various types, that they can surround them, constantly communicate with their ancestors, and that they can engage in time or dream travel. Coping with such a world requires organizations both for protection and placation. This mystical, magical, semi-animistic milieu underlies a number of belief systems, some of which are amongst the world's fastest growing.

But more importantly for the twenty-first century, these systems need to be understood for tolerance to increase. They should not be regarded as outdated relics of primitivism, but faiths that have something to offer the rest of us. What they have to offer are features that might help us to understand and to survive.

In this chapter we well discuss two examples. One is over a thousand years old, and has tendrils reaching into this century through descendents of the ancient Maya. The other has its roots in tribal Africa and flourishes today in the islands of the Caribbean, especially in Haiti, and along the coast of South America, especially northeast Brazil.

UTOPIA

In 1515 Thomas More was serving as the envoy to Flanders for Cardinal Wolsey, Lord Chancellor in the regime of the English King Henry VIII. Among other things, he gathered material for a book, which was published the following year. That book was entitled *Utopia*.

Lorraine Stobbart presents a fascinating, if unconventional, interpretation of this work in which she contends that More was actually describing Maya living in the Mexican Yucatan, not some fictional New World site.[1] Stobbart bolsters her theory with facts about Maya society and Spanish exploration. Maya society was supposedly "discovered" by three voyages beginning in 1518 and ending with Hernando Cortez a year later. However, there is ample evidence of prior contact.

The Caribbean and the Gulf of Mexico were peppered with explorers in the years following Columbus. The years 1510-1515 were ones of many trading and exploring voyages. Stobbart believes More learned of them in the English port of Bristol, in Bruges, or in Antwerp. Whether More wrote *Utopia* as a satire directed at his good friend Erasmus, or as an account of an actual society as described to him, it did contain many elements known to have been present in the Maya-Toltec city states then flourishing in the Yucatan.

The Yucatan Maya had inherited from their ancestors, the Guatemalan Maya of seven hundred years earlier, a belief system intimately involved with departed ancestors and omnipresent spirits. They were a technologically advanced people who were politically sophisticated, but their faith is what is of interest to our discussion.

Their faith was an intricate, artful blend of science and mysticism based upon a vibrant creation myth. The panoply of Maya deities was deeply enmeshed in every daily activity. A lunar calendar linked to planetary calculations produced a network of ritual lacquered with millennial concepts.

The people who became the Maya began to settle in the Petén lowlands of present day Guatemala, Belize, and Southern Mexico sometimes between 2500 and 2000 BCE. Their precise calendar pinpointed their origin at August 13, 3114 BCE. Anthropologists estimate that the people who became the Maya were winding their way down from North America through northern Mexico into Mesoamerica at about the same time.

These Maya created one of the world's great civilizations. Their polity was based upon city-states that were sometimes loosely linked in confederations and occasionally more tightly bound together under strong rulers, much as the Greeks had been. Although the Maya were noted for their urban culture, constructing some of the world's largest cities and tallest buildings, they were supplied by productive agronomics, which included raised-bed cultivation, crop rotation, and an irrigation system of canals connected to reservoirs. The population and agricultural production of the Petén, and then the Yucatan, has never again equaled what it was under the Maya.

The so-called Classic Maya period reached its apex around 900 CE, after flourishing for some seven hundred years. At that point, it mysteriously began to disintegrate from stresses eerily similar to those plaguing today's developed world – overpopulation relative to resources (especially water), pollution, and incessant warfare. Even though pockets of settlement remained scattered about the Petén, the bulk of the Maya abandoned once-great cities and migrated north into the Yucatan. Their civilization revived, mingled with the Toltec, and produced monuments such as Chichin-Iza. Upon the arrival of Cortez in 1520, smallpox and persecution began to decimate their culture. Subcutaneous vestiges survived and exist to this day under a Catholic veneer, still grounded in astronomy and magical spiritual connections.

The Maya astronomers and mathematicians invented the number zero before the Arabs or Indians. They used vigesimal number systems (based upon twenty) and calculated the orbit of their sacred planet Venus with an error factor of only 16 seconds per year. They only had three numerical symbols: one, five, and zero. Unlike our decimal system, which increases from left to right, the Maya vigesimal system increased from bottom to top. For quite some time it was believed that their system would only permit addition and subtraction, but recent research has uncovered evidence of complex multiplication and division as well.

The Maya calendar formed the mechanism of their belief system. It reached both backward to creation as we have seen, and forward to the predicted end of the world. In our terms this apocalypse will occur on October 15, 4772. Basically, the calendar functioned as if it were two different sized gears that meshed when they came into contact with each other. There was a 260-day lunar year consisting of thirteen 20-day months, and a 360-day solar year consisting of eighteen 20-day months. Appended to these constructs were five extremely unlucky adjustment days at year-end. Each day of each year had a name. The point where the calendars interlocked provided a special name, which would only occur once every fifty-two years, whose span was called a calendar round.

The millennial aspect of the calendar was taken from the solar year. The points of reference were multiples of twenty 20-day months. One 20-day multiple was a tun; twenty was a katun (7,200 days); four hundred was a baktun (144,000 days); eight thousand was a pictun (2,880,000 days).

These precise calculations fit into a mystical framework that worshipped animistic spirits, ancestors and unknown forces, employing complex ritual and hallucinogen-induced dream travel. There were multiple heavens and a lively underworld with which the Maya regularly interacted. Unlucky times at the end of c periods were surmounted by noble bloodletting and human sacrifice. Blood ensured renewal. When major calendric periods ended, the required ritual was longer and more severe. A baktun, for example, demanded months of cleansing. The end of the first pictun could only be survived by years of ceremonial purification. A Great Cycle would take 5,200 solar years (thirteen baktuns), and its end would mark a time when a corrupt and decadent world would undergo widespread destruction so that the symmetry and purity of its beginning could be restored. Translated into our calendar the first Maya Great Cycle will be completed on December 23, 2012. The completion of the second Great Cycle will mark the end of the world (26 baktuns, or 10,400 solar years from creation). As noted, that will occur on October 15, 4772.

As is evident, the Maya venerated regularity, symmetry, and predictability. Their belief system was based upon these attributes and the scientific expertise involved in their calculation. But the Maya were highly literate, frequently attending courses and lectures. They wrote profusely in hieroglyphics that were both syllabic and ideographic and able to express many nuances. The dialects of their spoken language, like Chinese, were different from their uniform writing.

For hundreds of years the Maya were an educated, articulate people who were capable of abstract intellectual pursuits as well as towering scientific accomplishments. At the same time, they worshipped multiple deities connected to animistic or spiritual forces and consulted their ancestors on every phase of decision-making. Their mystical, magical, millennial faith existed within a rigid framework. Inherent uncertainty was accommodated by ritual. The future's broad outlines were mathematically determined. And yet, as the Maya roamed the streets of their brilliantly colored, multi-storied rain-forest cities, a retinue of spirits that had to be acknowledged and appeased accompanied them.

The Maya were not the only civilization to accept a spirit world indistinguishable from daily life. However, they are an example of how an advanced society can be comfortable alongside a world of spirits. Maya beliefs are legitimate theological constructs, even when, as now, they flourish under the façade of another religion, such as Catholicism or Evangelical Protestantism. As such we should understand them, tolerate them, and perhaps learn from them.

THE LOA

In the Fon language *loa* is the word for spirits. Fon is spoken today in Togo and Benin, two small West African nations of the Volta River delta region nestled between Ghana and Nigeria. In the eighteenth century, many of the slaves who were shipped to the rich French island colony of Saint Dominique (now divided into the Dominican Republic and Haiti) came from the Volta River delta. They labored on the fabulously productive plantations that generated two-thirds of all French overseas trade and earned more than all of the American colonies combined. The descendants of these slaves comprise most of the population of present-day Haiti.

The belief system (loosely termed voudoun, or voodoo) especially prominent among Haiti's rural communities has its roots deep in the Volta delta and is in reality an intricate web of veneration of human and animistic spirits. The Haitian loa are everywhere, able to enter both living and dead humans only after an educated summons.

> Voudoun is abstracted from the day-to-day lives of the believers. In Haiti, as in Africa, there is no separation between the sacred and the secular, between the holy and the profane, between the material and the spiritual. Every dance, every song, every action is but a particle of the whole, each gesture a prayer for the survival of the entire community.[2]

In addition, this religion intimately connects believers with the sources of their awed worship. "Voudoun is a quintessentially democratic faith. Each believer not only has direct contact with the spirits, he actually receives them into his body."[3] The adept, or shaman, or in Haiti the houngan, acts as a translator, a theologian, who patiently uncovers complexities, but does not control access to the spirits. The hierarchy tiered beneath a houngan facilitates understanding rather that representing divinity. Like orthodoxy in any form, the belief system constructed around loa is comprehensive, consuming, and controlling. It is a way of life.

> For the Haitian, the ease with which the individual walks in and out of his spirit world is but a consequence of the remarkable dialogue that exists between man and the loa. The spirits are powerful and if offended can do great harm, but they are also predictable and if propitiated will gratefully provide all the benefits of health, fertility and prosperity. But just as man must honor the spirits, so the loa are dependant on man, for the human body is their receptacle.[4]

What is more, the health of each is vital to the health of the other. "In voudoun society, the physician is also the priest, for the condition of the spirit is as important as – and, in fact, determines – the physical state of the body."[5]

In Haiti, as in other cultures where spirits play a pivotal role, a complex but ordered world exists beneath an official form of religion (in this case Catholicism) and an official form of government (in this case a pale reflection of American-style democracy). The organization, operation, and power of the loa-centered society have little resemblance to what appears on the surface. Indeed, there is often a contradiction. Many government and corporate officials on the surface assume very different roles in the loa center. It is this characteristic which has traditionally made Haiti so difficult for outsiders to conquer, to occupy or to control. What is translucent for Haitians can be opaque for outsiders.

Some of the loa establishment are priest-interlocutors with specific duties and retinues devoted to the spirits. A more shadowy, and powerful, element is the Haitian version of the West African secret societies. They arrived with the eighteenth century slaves and have retained de facto control of the country ever since. These societies, and ones similar to them in other cultures, actually govern as theocracies.[6] Secrecy makes it extremely hard for the uninitiated observer to grasp the essence of the theocratic power structure.

A spirit oriented belief system can have an orthodox cadre that is effective but nearly invisible. This cadre provides its believers a worldview, a strictly ordered existence, and weapons to combat fears or uncertainties. It sets and enforces a social contract that is pervasively theocratic, albeit in an unusual form. Over two centuries in Haiti the spirit based belief system has provided foundation and structure to what often seems a chaotic society. It has sometimes provided the mechanism for repression, persecution, and even rebellion. It has always lived in the shadows, like the spirits it serves.

SUMMATION

While spirit based belief systems are only primitive in the sense that they deal directly with primal forces, most often they possess a sophisticated theological structure as well as a layered hierarchy. Too frequently, spirits are dismissed as some lower form of religious life. Many times they are concealed by the displayed belief system behind which they thrive. Spirit based belief lives on the two examples detailed above as it does in Brazil where devotion to the goddess Iemanja also reflects the ancient African faiths Umbanda and Candomble. The many examples of spirit worship that exist throughout the world are components making up our pantheon of faiths. In Europe and the United States immigrants with spirit-influenced belief systems are becoming a significant demographic factor. These belief systems provide answers about the cosmos fro many. They also glow from behind layers of faith more recently applied, but are no less valid in their own terms. As the world becomes more emotionally uncertain and intellectually complex, spirit-influenced belief systems may offer answers that comfort increasingly larger numbers of people.

---

[1] Lorraine Stobbart, *Utopia: Fact or Fiction? The Evidence from the Americas* (Gloucestershire: Alan Sutton Publishing, Ltd., 1992)

[2] Wade Davis, *The Serpent and the Rainbow*, (New York: Simon & Schuster, 985) p 76

[3] Ibid

[4] Ibid, p 218

[5] Ibid, p 222.

[6] For a discussion of secret society governing in Haiti see Michael Laguene's article "Bizango: A Voodoo Secret Society in Haiti:" contained in *Secrecy*, S. K. Tefft ed. (New York: Human Sciences Press, 1976)

Chapter Seven

Potentials

Let thy soul be as matter for all forms of beliefs.

Ibn al-Arabi

Whereas fate was central to Greeks and Romans,
hope is central to Jews and Christians.

Thomas Cahill
Sailing the Wine Dark Sea

The nature of belief has changed dramatically in recent years. Extremism has surfaced in more faiths in more locations than at any time since World War II. Dialogue between those who disagree has grown shrill where it exists at all. Religious policy and state policy are coming closer together in the Muslim world, the Indian sub-continent, and the United States. New faiths, or new offshoots of old faiths, are among the fastest growing belief systems. Fundamentalism, millennialism, and evangelicalism are words being heard with growing frequency. It would appear that a period of religious clashes with increasing intensity could constitute the foreseeable future.

But, maybe, there is some hope, as slim as it might seem at this moment. Perhaps dialogue can create understanding that in turn can spread tolerance. Perhaps out of religious sourced terror and waves of verbal arrows flying from one faith to another will come a realization that the path being taken is fraught with danger. Maybe, cultures and civilizations will, at the crucial moment pull back from the rim of the chasm into which they seem headed.

But perhaps the danger will not be realized in time, cooler heads will not prevail, and conflicts will grow in severity. Presently, this looks to be the more likely outcome. But even then, hope is not lost. As was the case in militant Greece of the sixth-century BCE or China's warring states period two centuries later, or the turbulent late Roman Empire, turmoil can give rise to sparkling creativity. Most great faiths have arisen from the ashes of such eras. Philosophy and the arts have often blossomed as swords were drawn and blood flowed. So, even if the coming decades are shrouded in pessimism, beneath the surface positive energy may be building to eventually enhance potentials.

TRENDS
Demographics

The richer nations, which comprise the industrial world, have populations that are aging and economic growth that is generally slowing. This combination is causing indigenous workforces to plateau in the United States, decline moderately in Great Britain, France, Germany and Scandinavia, and plunge by over a third in Italy and Japan. All of this will happen by mid century.[1]

What will also happen is that the social and financial infrastructure supporting these older populations will come under increasing pressure. By mid-century the over 65 group will amount to about 40% of the total United Sates population, versus 20% now, and in Japan the figure will be 50%, versus 20% now. Within the industrial nations the fastest rowing racial and ethnic groups will be non-European and non-white. This will make an explosive social and financial mix.

In the poorer nations the situation will be no less explosive, although in a very different way. In these countries populations are growing younger and more urban. In most less developed nations over 50% of the population is less than twenty years of age with high rates of unemployment. Moreover, they are pouring into cities. By 2015 urban areas in the developing world will hold 3.1 billion of the world's 4.1 billion city dwellers and 8 billion people. There will be at least 30 mega-cities of 10 million or more inhabitants in these poorer nations alone.

The infrastructure of these mega-cites will rapidly become largely non existent or non-functional unless some investments are made. Young unemployed people packed into cities with inadequate protection from disease or the elements will be under great pressure either to emigrate, revolt, or both. This will constitute a fertile breeding ground for any belief system that offers hope. Militant faiths or sects that promise change could find many takers in the endless poverty of third world mega-cities, and in the inner city slums of the industrial world. In fact, they already have.

In the industrial world, which has seen jobs and growth transferred overseas, an increased susceptibility to extremist militancy could lead to discrimination directed against recent immigrants or those with non-mainstream ethnicity.

These groups also will pose unwelcome competition for a weakening social welfare infrastructure. This, too, is already taking place. Religion has been thrust into the middle of the world's socio-economic problems because the belief systems of the disadvantage differ markedly from the mainstream establishment, which is often secular.

The progressively older developed world, the younger less developed world with more rapidly growing populations centered in cities, the pressures to migrate and against immigration, the accelerating increase of minority religions and ethnic groups in Europe and America, are all raising the likelihood of socio-economic disruptions. It has become depressingly obvious that these disruptions are at least partially fueled by religious extremism. Demographic trends seem to be encouraging extremist tendencies. Consequently, it is going to become progressively more urgent to establish the type of dialogue and understanding between belief systems that can strengthen moderation and marginalize extremism.

DIVISIONS AND RECONSTITUTIONS

Religions around the world are undergoing transformations, of which the highly publicized rise of fundamentalism is only a part. Let us take Christianity as an example. At the end of the twentieth century there were about 2.6 billion Christians in the world, compared to 1.2 billion as recently as 1970. Over that same thirty-year period, Christians in the United States grew from 81 million to 171 million.[2]

However, by the middle of the twenty-first century half of the world's Christians will be African and Latin American, with a further 20% being Asian. By that time the largest Christian population will still be in the United States, which will be followed in order, by Brazil, Mexico, Nigeria, Democratic Republic of Congo, Ethiopia and the Philippines. Non-Latin white Christians will account for only 20% of the global total. Clearly, these figures imply some changes in the character of the several Christian denominations, but the pure figures are only the tip of the iceberg.

Pentecostalism provides an example of Christian dynamics. There are almost half a billion of them worldwide, less than 10% of whom live in the United States. By 2040 some projections have them reaching 1 billion throughout the world. As it spreads rapidly this belief system can take different forms in different places, often acting as a thin veneer placed over an established faith.

Pentecostalism began as an offshoot of the Holiness movement in 1901 in Topeka, Kansas where Charles Fox Parham taught a Bible class. He constructed lessons based on the book of Acts, Chapter 2, verses 1-4. These verses reflected the early Christian belief that on the Jewish Feast of Weeks, 50 days after Passover, which they called Pentecost, the Holy Spirit descended upon the people permitting them to speak in other "tongues". Speaking in tongues, or glossolalia, has become a feature of Pentecostalism.[3] Having the Holy Spirit as a center of faith and reliance upon spiritual healing are other features.

In 1906, William J. Seymour, an African-American evangelist, started a mission in Los Angeles for the group Parham had originally called Apostolic Faith. Seymour's mission took hold and grew. Today, at least two-thirds of the Pentecostals in this country are African-American, but the faith's main growth has come from overseas, particularly from Latin America and sub-Saharan Africa.

The features of modern Pentecostalism are relatively standard, although the exact forms may vary. There is a deep personal connection to the Holy Spirit. Prophecy, exorcism, and spiritual healing are prevalent. Obedience to spiritual authority by a mystical, puritanical community that supports material success is common. Closeness to the type of spirit worlds we visited in the previous chapter is evident in Pentecostal belief. This belief has appealed to just the type of poor first generation urban dweller that has become prevalent throughout the less developed world.

The relevance of this movement is that it represents a significant trend. Populist, largely conservative, mystical, millennial believers are becoming more numerous. They follow scripture closely[4]. They look back to the early Christian Church for guidance, proselytize vigorously, and place great store in basic values. These features are part of a trend, of which Pentecostalism is only one representative, which is not confined to a single faith. It is likely to flourish for many years to come with the world's belief systems growing more conservative, more charismatic, and more evangelical.

FUNDAMENTALISM

Fundamentalism is a word that has been regularly in the media during this century. It has been applied to many aspects of belief without a general understanding about what it means. Ironically, an effort called the Fundamentalism Project that involved some of this country's most eminent scholars published its first volume in 1991. The fifth volume came out in 1996. A summary work called *Strong Religion* was published in 2003.

This comprehensive study looked at fundamentalism in all major faiths in every part of the globe. With such an exhaustive work at its fingertips it might seem that our government, and other governments would be able to understand the phenomenon of fundamentalism when it sprang upon them. Sadly, this does not appear to be the case. All of us tend to group fundamentalists together, often stigmatizing them. This happens even though fundamentalism is a thriving part of every faith, and has been for centuries.

At the end of the nineteenth century certain Protestants began to call themselves Fundamentalists signifying their rejection of Darwin's theory of evolution, and other scientific principles. They made five points the core of their belief: 1) the absolute accuracy of the Bible; 2) the divinity of Jesus Christ; 3) the Virgin Birth of Jesus Christ; 4) acceptance of the fact that Jesus Christ died as an Atonement for the sins of the world; and 5) acceptance of the physical resurrection of Jesus Christ and his bodily return to earth on the Last Day.

Protestant fundamentalism received international notoriety during the trial of John Thompson Scopes in July of 1925. Scopes was a high school biology teacher in Tennessee who was prosecuted for teaching evolution with public money. Three-time presidential candidate William Jennings Bryan aided the prosecution and Clarence Darrow provided the defense. Scopes was convicted, given a nominal fine, and exonerated by an appeals court. Fundamentalism then faded from the public consciousness in this country for about fifty years. But, by the 1980s and 1990s it was back, fighting against secular humanism, which was seen as an attempt by science to subvert religion.

Of course, what became called fundamentalism was not new to Western civilization in the late nineteenth century. Nor has it been the exclusive property of the West. It has existed at many times in many places under many names, but displaying similar characteristics. Western fundamentalism burst out of the Middle Ages and the Reformation to thrive among the Protestant sects of England, Scotland, Switzerland, and to some degree Holland, of the sixteenth and seventeenth centuries. They played a significant role in overthrowing King Charles I of England in the 1640s. Millennial, evangelical fundamentalism came to New England at about the same time.

Separatist Congregationalists who wanted to escape hierarchies or connections to other congregations, were the initial, puritanical settlers of New England. There was a pre-Revolutionary fundamental blossoming in Connecticut and Massachusetts called the Great Awakening, which was led by Congregational minister Jonathan Edwards. Revivalist Charles Grandison Finney led a Second Great Awakening in the 1830s and 1840s. It started in upstate New York, a fundamentalist breeding ground, and spread like wildfire through the Northeast and late twentieth century surges pushed always-prevalent fundamental belief to new heights and new visibility.

Several words have become associated with American fundamentalism. *Evangelical*, denotes a strict, specific following of the teachings of the Gospel, written accounts of the life and teachings of Jesus Christ. *Charismatic* means religious or emotional spontaneity. *Millennial* refers to the 1000 year reign of Jesus Christ which will descend upon earth and its sincere believers following an apocalyptic event. *Born-Again* is a conversion or renewed commitment to Jesus Christ as one's personal savior. These characteristics apply across a wide variety of sects and systems. They are evident in independent churches or in the congregations of televangelists.

A Gallup poll taken in December 2002 showed that 46% of all adult Americans described themselves as *born again* or *evangelical*, 58% said they believed in evolution as the sole explanation, and 68% said that they believed in the devil.[5] According to the Christian Booksellers Association evangelical publishing accounts for $2 billion of the annual $13 billion of the general book sales. In 2003 and 2004 *The Purpose Driven Life* by Rick Warren sold 15 million copies. The eleven novels based upon the Book of Revelations written by Dr. Timothy La Haye and Jerry Jenkins have sold over 60 million copies in the 10 years since the first volume came on the market.

Fundamental Christianity has thus become a potent economic, social, and political force in twenty-first century America. Every day we see evidence of this in the national media. Our fundamentalists are reaching across the globe to proselytize, with great success. Christian Zionists have provided strong political and financial support to the state of Israel, especially to the West Bank settlers. Fundamental Christianity is not only alive in the United States it is growing.

The type of religious fundamentalism we in this country most closely associate with violence are two Sunni Islamic sects, the Wahhabis of Saudi Arabia and their first cousins the Deobandis of Pakistan. They are only one segment of Islam, but even so are far from the monoliths we tend to perceive.[6] Let us take a look at how they arose and expanded.

Muhammad ibn Abd al-Wahhab (1703-1792 CE) was born in the north central part of what is now Saudi Arabia. He became a radical reformer of what he considered misguided Islam, acting in the tradition of fourteenth century Damascene ibn Taymiyyah, who himself has become a role model for modern Sunni fundamentalists. Wahhabi hoped to revive Islam by eradicating the layers of judiciary with their interpretations and returning to the literal meaning of the Quran and the hadiths, which were sayings of the Prophet recorded by his closest associates. Wahhab received support from the head of the Saud family, the present rulers of Saudi Arabia, who used his doctrines to enhance their popular support and move from regional tribal leaders to national monarchs.

Modern Wahhabism, the state religion of Saudi Arabia, was re-energized by the words of Cairene Rashid Rida. Rida saw Islam threatened by the values of the imperial West and advocated not only a return to fundamental texts but also government by Sharia, which is Islamic law. Inspired by Taymiyyah, founded by Wahhabi and refreshed by Rida this sect, funded by the proceeds from pumping oil, has established a worldwide presence. We see its face most often as Osama bin Laden, a believer, and the words of firebrand clerics. This is its most aggressive face, but not its only one. There are pacific believers as well.

Followers of Wahhab in India established a sect in 1867 at the city of Deoband. The sect flourished as a center for dispensing the teachings of Wahhab. In the 1930s an Indian Muslim by the name of Maulana Maududi, and an Egyptian Sayyid Qutb about a decade later, inflamed the Deobandis with calls for a purge of western influence and the establishment of a theocratic state. Their ideas were influential in the founding of Pakistan.

Today the fundamentalist, puritanical Deobandis operate an estimated 30,000 madrassas, schools devoted to studying the Quran, in Pakistan. One of their offshoots is the Taliban (talibs are students) who drew their followers from Deobandi madrassas.

Other militant fundamentalists exist in many countries with basically the same purpose, force a return to what they perceive as religious basics. However, fundamentalists are not inherently militant or repressive. The strict nature of their beliefs often precludes acceptance of other systems and makes tolerance difficult. But as our own national history has shown, fundamentalism can become a peaceful, positive force. It is a worthy objective for people to attempt a level of understanding that can retain and expand this positivity.

CROSSROADS

It would be encouraging to think that we have reached a crossroad where some of the available paths lead away from religious military toward tolerance. Hugh Heclo makes a statement about the current climate of belief in the United States that lends support to this hope.

> To claim that there are absolute moral truths (a view rejected by three out of four American adults at the end of the twentieth century), or that one religious faith is more valid than another, is widely regarded as a kind of spiritual racism. The new cornerstone of belief is that moral truths depend on what individuals choose to believe relative to their particular circumstances. Human choice has become the trump, value and judgmentalism the chief sin. Thus, three-fourths of the large majority of American society who want religion say it does not matter which religion becomes more influential.[7]

If this observation proves to be accurate, it could signal the development of a more spiritual, but less religiously confrontational society. There are, of course, those who disagree. However, there is at least potential that the path that our nation will take could be a favorable one. A couple of examples from history illustrate how relative tolerance can flourish, even between eras of repression.

AL-ANDALUS

For two and one half centuries (775 to 1002 CE) a remarkably accomplished society of Muslims, Christians and Jews (under Muslim rule was both prosperous and cultured. An Umayyad prince named Abd- al-Rahman set up his capitol in Cordoba and founded a dynasty.

The unique blend of cultures that thrived in the loosely ruled collection of Iberian city-states created a cosmopolitan interaction. This interaction produced world famous artistic, educational, scientific, and economic results. The creative energy ignited was as bright as ever existed anywhere. Medicine leapt forward. The work of the classic Greeks was translated and thus recovered. Mathematics reached new heights. Astronomy expanded its purview. Poetry was luxuriant. Scholars from all over flocked to learn.

Eventually dynastic enervation coupled with fundamentalist invasions, Muslims from North Africa, Christians from across the Pyrenees, gradually snuffed out the creative light. While it existed al-Andalus demonstrated what relative tolerance could bring forth.

THE AGE OF AKBAR

The first Moghul ruler of India was Babur, a descendent of Tamerlane.[8] He was driven from his home city in Central Asia, but came south with some followers. Babur conquered Kabul in 1504 CE Lahore in 1520 and Delhi in 1526, thus creating what became known as the Mogul Empire. The empire was ruled by Muslims, but was mainly Hindu. It lasted for 350 years until the British conquered the peninsula.

Akbar was the grandson of Babur and the third Mogul emperor who ruled from 1556 to 1605. Upon his father's untimely death, he ascended the throne at the age of 13. For the first six years he was under the influence of Bayram Khan, a successful general, and military expansion was the theme. By 19 Akbar was prepared to take over full control for himself and begin to move in a different direction.

While Akbar proved to be an outstanding general and administrator, laying the foundation for the empire's greatness, it was in the field of religion that he is of most interest to us. He read, consulted, and discoursed. One of his favorite activities was to wander among his subjects, often in disguise, seeking their opinions on belief.[9] He also convened a council that was directed to explore all possibilities for spiritual enlightenment. This council included members from many faiths, including Catholic priests from the Portuese colony of Goa.

Ideas generated by the council led to the formation of a new monotheistic faith. It was centered up on the semi-deified emperor and was called Din Ihahi (Divine Faith). Devine Faith was essentially mystical, but contained elements gleaned from Islam, Hinduism, Zoroastrianism and Christianity. Two of the greatest influences on Akbar's thinking were the Sufi Kabin (alive during his reign) and Guru Namok founder of the Sikh religion, itself a blend of Hindu and Islamic elements, (who died seventeen years prior to the emperor's birth). Both Kabin and Namok advocated unity of the godhead and equality among believers.

Akbar abolished discriminatory religious taxes. He augmented the Central Asian nobility with members from other faiths and ethnic groups. He established an inclusive policy towards all belief systems. In all of these actions he was opposed by the conservative Muslim clergy, who eventually triumphed as Akbar's successors, were progressively more strict and orthodox in their observance of Islam. However brief, Akbar's pursuit of tolerance can serve as an inspiration to a world also attempting to cope with complex matters of faith.

DIRECTIONS

After the last Great Awakening at the end of the 19th century, liberal theology made steady gains in all the mainline American churches. By the 1950s it represented the consensus within Protestantism, and was also softening the edges of American Catholicism and Judaism. Yet it seems now to have entered a period of decline. Over the past 30 years we have seen the erosion of traditional mainstream faiths and the upsurge of evangelical, Pentecostal, charismatic and 'neo-orthodox' movements. This trend towards conservatism is evident not only among Protestants but among Catholics and Jews as well. Politics played a large role in this, especially divisions over the Vietnam War and the cultural transformations since the 1960s. But the deepest dynamics were spiritual. They have been driven by the need for structure created by an unfettered, complex society suddenly experiencing geographical fallout.

It appears that there are limits to the liberalization of biblical religion. The more the Bible is treated as a historic document, the more its message is interpreted in universalist terms, the more that churches sanctify the political and cultural order, the less hold the liberal region will eventually have on the hearts and minds of believers. This dynamic is particularly pronounced in Protestantism, which heightens the theological tension brought on by being in the world but not of it. Liberal religion imagines a pacific order in which good citizenship, good morals, and rational beliefs co-exist harmoniously. It is therefore unprepared when the messianic and eschatological forces of texts following faith begin to oppose the current societal condition.

The leading thinkers of the British and American enlightenments hoped that life in a modern democratic order would shift the focus of Christianity from a faith-based reality to a reality-based faith. For periods of time in our history it has done exactly that. But American religion is moving in the opposite direction today, back toward the ecstatic, literalist and evangelical spirit of the Great Awakenings. Its most unsettling manifestations are not political yet rather they are cultural.[10]

A poll taken by the Associated Press and Ipsos in May of 2005 found that in the United States 61% of those surveyed said religious leaders should not influence government decisions. But 39% said religious leaders should sway policy makers, by far the highest percentage of any country surveyed. The others were Australia, Britain, Canada, France, Germany, Italy, Mexico, South Korea, and Spain. The fact that almost half of our citizens think that religion should be a part of politics, and government is pointing in that direction, promises to alter our social contract if it persists.

The types of faith that are growing here and around the world do not seem particularly receptive to tolerance. To be sure, there are a few byways going in a more favorable direction, and possibly they may multiply with time. An Iranian reformer spoke for many around the world when he voiced these sentiments. "No one is perfect enough to have an absolute claim on understanding the truth. And no single understanding of Islam is automatically more correct or definitive than another."[11] But he seems to be an exception, particularly in Iran.

With Islamic militancy growing in Europe, Hindu nationalism India, and fundamentalists with extreme views attaining increased visibility in other locations, the outlook for moderation, at least in the near term, appears less than bright. Terrorism has hardened attitudes towards belief and promoted fortified enclaves. Governmental inclusion of religious issues in its policy-making, the headscarf wearing by French Muslim female schoolchildren or faith based social policies are examples, appears to be on the increase. For all of these reasons, and more, the world currently does not seem to be taking the path that leads towards greater religious tolerance. In the next chapter we will take a look at some of the ways this trend might be reversed.

---

[1] Sources for the figures used in this section are the United Nations and the United States Census Bureau.

[2] Figures on Christianity are from the *World Christian Encyclopedia*. For the purposes of this analysis Mormons are considered Christians. Not every theologian agrees.

[3] In the first century C. E., Saint Paul found the Corinthian Christians speaking in languages, or tongues, that were meant to echo the outpouring of the Holy Spirit at

Pentecost. Their speech was called glossolalia after the Greek words for tongue; *glossa*, and for speaking; *lalia*. A concise description of this belief and its development can be found in *The Faith: A History of Christianity*, by Brian Moynahan, and published by Doubleday in 2002.

[4] Jaroslav Pelikan in his book *Whose Bible Is It? A History of Scripture throughout the Ages*, (New York: Viking, 2005) provides an interesting account of the evolution of the Bible over the centuries.

[5] An interesting discussion of these factors can be found in two books: James M. Ault, Jr., *Spirit and Flesh: Life in a Fundamentalist Baptist Church*, (New York: Alfred A. Knopf, 2004) and Christian Smith, *Christian America? What Evangelicals Really Want*, (Berkley: University of California Press, 2000).

[6] Natana J. Delong-Bas in *Wahhabi Islam: From Revival to Reform to Global Jihad*, (New York: Oxford University Press, 2004) makes this point along with an in depth history.

[7] Hugh Heclo and Wilfred M. McClay, eds., *Religion Returns to Public Square: Faith and Policy in America*, (Princeton: Woodrow Wilson Center Press and Johns Hopkins Press, 2003).

[8] The word Moghul means Mongol in Hindu. Among the accepted spellings are Moghal, Moaghul, and Moghul.

[9] This and other subjects are covered in his diary *The Babur-nama*, which can be read in its English translation by A. S. Beveridge, published in London in 1921.

[10] Mark Lilla wrote an essay entitled "Church Meets State" for the *New York Times Book Review* of May 15, 2005, page 39, from which these sentiments are taken.

[11] Adul Karim Soroush (born Hussein Dabbagh) as quoted in Robin Wright's *The Last Great Revolution: Turmoil and Transformation in Iran*, (New York: Alfred A. Knopf, 2000) p. 52.

Chapter Eight

Bridges

How much more in accord with Christ's teaching it is to regard the whole world as one household...think of all mankind as brethren...not to examine where a man lives but how well he lives.

Erasmus

I do not consider it a given that people can only validate their beliefs by invalidating the beliefs of others. I do not accept the conclusion that matters of religion have to produce exclusion, discrimination, or persecution. I believe that intolerance can be diverted by dialogue and understanding. I look upon the millions that have died over the years in the name of religion as an unmitigated tragedy. I am convinced that there is another alternative, another direction. I call it "bridges".

Maya Angelou, the African-American author spoke of bridges at her seventy-fifth birthday celebration on February 10, 2004.

Men, yes Women, yes. Children, black and white, yes. I have something to say about being a human being, who we really are and really can be, that we can be more than we appear. If we believed, if we trusted, if we had the courage to step outside the box and smile at someone of a different color, someone who calls God by a different name – just a little bit of that can make a difference.

If we learn about each other as human beings, not merely stereotypes, intolerance becomes harder to practice. If we work to reinforce moderation in our overt actions, extremism will have a harder time spreading. If we realize that neither decisiveness nor clarity requires ruthlessness or disrespect, persecution will not have the environment in which to grow. Forgiveness, volunteerism, and democratic dialogue are specific examples of these bridges.

FORGIVENESS

Challenges are a part of life and are to be expected. Being a prisoner of fear or existing without hope is a tragedy. The essential quality of life can be enhanced if societies practiced an attribute that is at the core of virtually every belief system – *forgiveness.*

It should be woven into our daily lives, and into our dreams for the future, but the perceived need for revenge too often crowds it out. The lust for retribution is a condition unfortunate enough by itself but doubly pernicious when it undermines the very principles for which we purport to stand. If revenge becomes societal, cultural, or civilizational, the damage vengeance could cause becomes considerable.

Forgiveness can be very hard to put into practice as it encounters the frictions of day-to-day existence. Resentments can scar families, friends, and associates. Instinctive reactions can succumb to the lure of surface impulses, rendering deeper, more meaningful emotions harder to tap. People can avoid this seductive morass if there are beacons in place to guide them.

One of the most remarkable, if not often acknowledged political creations of the twentieth century was conceived in 1995. It was only one year after Nelson Mandela become South Africa's fist black president that he and Archbishop Desmond Tutu organized the Truth and Reconciliation Commission (TRC). The aim of this body was to facilitate the peaceful reconstitution of a society that had been shredded by the vicious racial repression enacted through the policy of apartheid. The TRC proposed to accomplish this feat by employing a revolutionary strategy. They elevated forgiveness to the level of national policy. This policy offered forgiveness, not revenge, as the primary means to obtain closure, if the confessions received were deemed to be sincere.

While the TRC did not provide a perfect solution, and forgiveness was not the only reason, the transition to a black majority government took place with far less than the anticipated level of violence. More importantly, forgiveness was transformed into empowerment and healing for both individuals and groups of victims.

One of the commission's members a psychologist named Pumla Gobido-Madikizela articulated the reasons why the quality of forgiveness is a valuable addition to any social contract.

> One of the challenges a political community faces in seeking to make the transition into a properly functioning democracy is therefore to create conditions that encourage replacing enmity with, if not friendship, then at least regard for others as fellow humans. For the absence of empathy, whether at the communal or personal level, signals a condition that, in subtle but deeply destructive ways, separates people from one another.[1]

Forgiveness can also be an ethical duty that we owe to ourselves as members of a community.[2] This duty may not involve forgetting, but rather a conscious decision to overcome resentment. It is the deliberate nature of this act that empowers the forgiver and cements the community.

> Forgiveness is about reclaiming and giving dignity to one's memory through the acknowledgement of terrible acts done. It is revenge on a higher level – I will not retain the hatred you sowed me. I will not stoop to the level that you did. For the victims it is a moment of empowerment. The victim now has the power to grant or refuse what the perpetrator desperately needs. It does diminish us when we insist upon a vengeful response. When we reach out with empathy, we are doing what the perpetrator was unable to do. Whenever evil occurs, someone somewhere must stop the cycles of violence, and must stoop the cycles of evil.[3]

As we go about the ordinary business of living and our nation exerts its influence upon the world, forgiveness properly employed can temper the harshness of vengeful certainty. Forgiveness can inject the true spirit of God into human activities. By so doing it can be a bridge to peace through tolerance and respect.

VOLUNTEERISM

In the United States almost 60 million people volunteer every year.[4] That figure constitutes almost 28% of the over-16 population. However, volunteering, which has always been an American trademark, has faced economic challenges recently. Our economy changed from regular manufacturing shifts to an irregular, service-dominated workplace. Times for volunteers had to be made less rigid. Meetings had to be made more flexible. Many households now have two working adults. Accommodations by organizations have been necessary to permit them to attract volunteers. Budgets for non-profit and government entities have been under pressure making volunteers more of an economic necessity, especially in the provision of social services. Integrating time into the mechanics of organizations has required policy adjustments.

Beyond these economic challenges, volunteering has grown even more critical for the preservation of our social fabric. It offers an opportunity to come in to contact with people who may appear differently, act differently and believe differently. Volunteering allows people to see each other as human beings and opens channels for relating. It can bring us out of our chosen enclaves and habitual routes, thereby lessening the sting of resentment arising from disagreement with unfamiliar ideas and increasing the potential for understanding between various groups.

The American Jewish World Services provides one example of how volunteering can bring separate areas closer together. In this case the differing elements belonged to one faith, Judaism. The organization funds, offers technology, and attracts volunteers to 175 projects in 40 countries. This is unquestionably important for the recipients. But the biggest beneficiaries may be the volunteers themselves. They come from all four branches of contemporary Judaism: Orthodox; Conservative; Reform, and Reconstructionist. To be effective, the volunteers have to work together despite their different rules and rituals. They have to respect one another's habits and expressions in order to provide their services.

Anne Brenner who practices Reform Judaism and is a student from Los Angeles comments on working with Orthodox volunteers. "It was not hard, because of the generosity that the Orthodox young men had shown."[5] The organization attempts to follow the mandate *tikkun olam*, which means repair the world. This principle applies as much to the volunteers themselves as it does to interactions between them and the people they serve. Their experience "was a visible statement of a Jewish understanding of moral duty and human solidarity. It promised an enrichment of the Jewish community."[6]

A seventeen-year-old woman from the Boston area describes her experiences with volunteers from the House of David Surfriders, a quasi-religious organization founded in 1999 which provides volunteers to work with troubled teenagers. "You usually don't get something for nothing. Most places you go for religion they say, 'you must believe this'. If you believe something else, you're wrong. Here everyone shares views. They listen. It's not preaching God all the time."[7]

Volunteering also promotes compassion, which is a basic part of virtually every faith. Those who serve people in need are able to witness a daily struggle to overcome adversity. People who are in pain or near death accept compassion, but they also give it. Volunteers can be the beneficiaries, as can their values.

By volunteering different perspectives can intersect at nodes of comprehension. The mere existences of these nodes can impede the progress of intolerance. Volunteerism is an important bridge for us to learn about each other. Learning will breed understanding, which in turn has an excellent chance for leading to tolerance. Hopefully, volunteering will continue to expand.

DEMOCRATIC DIALOGUE

Democracy is certainly not the most efficient or responsive form of government. Both the slowly turning wheels of bureaucracy, and the fallout from political activities, can clog its mechanism. However, there is one priceless feature of democracy, which is that it facilitates dialogue.

We who live in democracies are free to talk to one another about any subject. We have numerous institutions specifically designed to facilitate dialogue. However, many faiths are not democracies. While theological debate is as old as recorded history, it is not always encouraged, and can be specifically prohibited, even in democracies.

Democratic dialogue is communications between equals. It is conducted with respect for, if not agreement with, other opinions. Questioning, listening, discussing are all a part of it. Solutions are not required from democratic dialogue. But receiving the feeling that one's opinions count and the creation of venues for open exchange are necessary. In that way dialogue can be a safety valve as well as a vehicle.

Religion has not been very adept at generating such an environment. Sensitivities, desire for unshakable convictions, and threats perceived from any questioning have blocked democratic dialogue in religion. For effective bridges to be built this condition has to change. Sometimes acknowledging that key differences of opinion exist but making agreements not to debate them is the best bridge that can be built.[8]

Talking *with* people can be a substitute for talking *at* people. Comprehension can replace fear. The situation within and between faiths leaves a great deal to be desired all over the globe. Bridges are urgently needed. Democratic dialogue could be one of those. Interfaith groups are making shifts in this direction, but even more effort is needed.

BRIDGES TO THE EXTREMES

No discussion of bridges would be complete without an effort to see how religious extremism could be reached by moderation, and at least partially defused. Obviously, the task will be difficult, and the rate of success, at least initially, could be low. But when believers are blowing themselves up amid crowds of civilians in the name of God and killing in the name of faith, extremism is occurring in other ways and the attempt has to be made.[9]

The most militant extremists are always going to be difficult to get into the same room with, much less conduct a dialogue. But the hard liners who fit into this category are relatively few in number. The aim of bridges has to be expanding the ranks of moderates, and keeping as many as possible from becoming intractable hard liners.

In this quest there is some hope. Both Hamas and the Islamic Brotherhood, for example, have branches that provide a wide range of social services in areas where such services are not readily available. Perhaps bridges can be built to these sectors. Much of the Irish Republican Army was brought back from the brink of interminable violence and moved toward some type of communal interaction largely through contact with its less militant extremes. Dialogue and contact with less militant portions of extremist groups are successfully ongoing in India, Pakistan, the Philippines, Indonesia, and Sri Lanka. There is hope that these can be expanded.

Not all bridges will be successful, but extermination policies are less likely, history has shown, if contacts proliferate. Intolerance pushes people toward extremes it does not reclaim them. We can ask ourselves whether it does any good to interact with a fundamentalist who is convinced that he or she is correct and that you are hopelessly wrong in matters of belief. The answer has to be that contact is always worth the effort. The results might disappoint, but the attempt is worthy if it deters even one person from engaging in discrimination, repression or violence.

The path to violence, with its usual detour towards revenge, tends to be irreversible. At the same time, I am convinced that the vast majority of human beings are reluctant to travel it. Even obdurate believers, obsessed with textual purity and constrained by the strictures of their faith, would like to avoid this path if at all possible. That reluctance leaves some room, however slight the opening might be, for bridges to be built. The critical bridges are not so much to keep the hard line extremists from acting in militantly extreme manner, that is a long shot, although one worth attempting. The critical bridges are the ones that keep moderates and non-militant extremists from supporting or condoning militancy. These are bridges that surely can be built, and their key raw material is humanitarian respect.

CONCLUSION

There are some things I like to contemplate when I fear that Satan's cauldron is bubbling ominously. They give me comfort when I realize that human beings are suffering under intolerant structures and when incendiary words spew from the mouths or pens of leaders. I am aware that the pressures of extremism seem to be increasing, but violent persecution is not an inevitable outcome and intolerance can be diverted. I believe this deeply. Even as forces gather in mutual menace, I retain hope and optimism that humanity will eventually triumph.

One of these contemplated things is at the core of Daoism

> The central focus of the Daoist way of thinking is the decisive role of deference in the establishment and preservation of relationships...Deference involves a yielding (and being yielded to) grounded in an acknowledgement of the shared excellence of particular loci in the process of one's own self-cultivation. Deferential acts require that one put oneself literally in the place of the other, and in so doing, incorporate what was the object of deference into what is one's own developing disposition. And one's own disposition thus fortified becomes available as a locus of deference for others.[10]

"Accommodation, far from being passive or weak, is the source of the fullness of strength and influence, timeliness and efficacy. Indeed, accommodation is inclusionary, enabling one to extend oneself through patterns of deference."[11]

The concept of strength through deference-accommodation is intriguing. It is by no means easy to employ, but the results could be electric if it ever caught on. I am drawn to it as an alternative to confrontation and the escalating emotions that induces. While not part of the western tradition, except for sayings like: "Do unto others as you would have them do unto you", this concept should be explored, and tested, further. The great thirteenth century poet and philosopher Jalaluddin Rumi (1207-1273 CE) put this thought beautifully. "Many of the faults you see in others, dear reader, are your own nature reflected in them."[12]

Light bathes everything it touches in its all-embracing glow. Light plays a major role in many faiths, often representing divinity with its purity and brilliance. Light has been scientifically proven to improve disposition, just as its deprivation induces depression.

Whether soft or acute, whether bright or dim, light is actually a compendium of colors and refractions. The brittle blue light bouncing off of an iceberg or the softly humid rays filtering through the leaves of a rain forest are all embracing. Light is ecumenical in its envelopment, as the following description of its composition makes clear.

> If you require any demonstration of the fact that colors have no physical embodiment, take a piece of while paper and a glass prism. Then hold the latter so that it catches a ray of direct sunlight. The white ray of sunlight through the prism is spread out upon the white paper as a multicolored band, with red at one end and violet at the other. Where do these colors come from? They appear because each ray of light producing them has its own angle of refraction, and is bent accordingly as it passes through the prism.[13]

There are many colors and angles of refraction in the area of belief. Light rays provide an example of how they can combine to produce a unified effect. Contemplating the effects of light gives me hope that as it surmounts what appear to be unbridgeable canyons, we humans can eventually attain peaceful understanding.

Obstacles remain stacked in the way of implementing these idealistic concepts. But many of them can be removed. We have seen that science need not be an impediment to belief. We have noted that the somewhat fluid nature of evolving truth can lend itself to benign adjustments, if earnestly desired. We have observed that similarities among faiths outweigh differences. There are numerous cogent proposals for building bridges across daunting ideological chasms.[14] Thus, there is no shortage of ideas. What there may be a shortage of is will. If the will to build bridges should develop, collective energies and intellects can produce a positive result, and the prospects for religious tolerance would be enhanced. This result cannot be achieved unless individual believers, groups of believers and faith-based organizations become actively engaged in slowing the worldwide drift of religious moderates towards supporting or condoning extremism. I firmly believe that people can be guided towards bridges, for it is their natural, basic instinct. A glance at the founding principles of any faith reinforces this belief.

---

[1] Pumla Gobodo-Madikizela, *A Human Being Died That Night: A South African Story of Forgiveness*, (New York: Houghton Mifflin, 2003) p. 127.

[2] Avishai Margalit expressed this view in his book, *The Ethics of Memory*, (Cambridge: Harvard University Press, 2003).

[3] Reneé Graham, *The Boston Globe*, February 25, 2003, quoting Pumla Godobo-Madikizela.

[4] Statistics are from the United States Labor Dept.

[5] Peter Steinfels, "Beliefs", *The New York Times*, January 17, 2004.

[6] Ibid.

[7] Tina Cassidy. "Catching the Big One", *The Boston Globe*, August 24, 2002.

[8] In her book God on the Quad, (New York: St. Martin's Press, 2005), Naomi Schaefer Riley gives and encouraging picture of students at faith-based colleges. Her work found them largely willing to be tolerant and inclusive while firmly adhering to their beliefs.

[9] Michael P. Lynch makes this point throughout his book, *True To Life: Why Truth Matters*, (Cambridge: The MIT Press, 2005)

[10] *Dao De Jing: A Philosophical Translation*, translated and with commentary by Roger Ames and David L. Hall, (New York: Ballantine Books, 2003) p. 38

[11] Ibid, p. 101.

[12] This quote from Rumi's masterpiece *Mathnawi* is presented in *The Rumi Collection*, selected and edited by Kabin Helminski and published in Boston by Shambala in 2000. The quote is found on page 18.

[13] F. F. Rockwell and Esther C. Grayson, *The Complete Book of Flower Arrangement*, (New York: The American Garden Guild, Inc. and Doubleday & Co., Inc., 1947) p. 42.

[14] "Noah Feldbaum has made some suggestions to close the divide between religiously motivated political positions in his book, *Divided by God: The Church-States Problem and What We Should Do About It*, (New York: Farrar, Strauss & Giroux, 2005).

Index